— THE —
PILGRIM JOURNEY

— THE —
PILGRIM JOURNEY

A History of Pilgrimage in the Western World

JAMES HARPUR

BlueBridge

Parts of this book were first published as *Sacred Tracks*.

Published by
B l u e B r i d g e
An imprint of
United Tribes Media Inc.
Katonah, New York

www.bluebridgebooks.com

ISBN: 9781629190006

Library of Congress Control Number: 2016932605

Cover design by Cynthia Dunne
Cover image top: Duncan McKenzie / Getty Images
Cover image bottom: Pilgrims who travel to Canterbury (13th century), choir window,
Canterbury Cathedral / De Agostini Picture Library / G. Dagli Orti / Bridgeman Images
Text design by Cynthia Dunne

Printed in the United States of America

10 9 8 7 6 5 4 3 2 1

CONTENTS

INTRODUCTION

"The longest journey begins with a single step."

Laozi

In the early twenty-first century, pilgrimage in the West is enjoying a boom, perhaps more so than at any time since the Middle Ages. Shrines such as Lourdes in France, Santiago de Compostela in Spain, and the basilicas of Our Lady of Guadalupe in Mexico and Sainte-Anne-de-Beaupré in Canada receive millions of pilgrims every year. At the heart of this attraction is a spiritual impulse that has existed from time immemorial. It is a desire that connects us with our medieval forebears and, indeed, ancient ancestors, and which in turn will connect us with our descendants. Pilgrims of every era and every faith are bonded by comparable aspirations, hopes, doubts, physical endeavors, rituals, and prayers.

The reasons for pilgrimage are numerous. They include giving thanks to God, fulfilling a vow, petitioning a holy figure for a cure, performing a penance, reinvigorating one's faith, and, more unofficially, experiencing the sights and sounds of the journey. A pilgrimage also traditionally has a number of recognized stages: preparation, including putting one's affairs in order before departing and acquiring the right traveling clothes and accessories; the journey itself; the arrival, accompanied by sacred rituals (such as saying prayers and lighting a candle); the return journey; and reintegration into the world the pilgrim had left behind.

It is these stages and rituals that have created a coherent pilgrimage tradition down the ages. To take just one example: contemporary pilgrims often leave at a shrine ex-voto offerings—symbolic tokens of the physical ailments from which they hope to be delivered or have been delivered, for example an image of an eye or a leg. Tokens of gratitude were also left by ancient Greek visitors at the healing sanctuary of the god Asclepius at Epidaurus, long before the time of Christ. And they were a staple of medieval pilgrimage. For instance, in Exeter Cathedral in southwest England, the masonry above the tomb of a fifteenth-century bishop named Edmund Lacy was damaged (in 1942, during World War II) and revealed a cache of wax votive offerings—miniature models of arms, legs, feet, and torsos left by medieval pilgrims to show which parts of their bodies had been healed. Ex-votos are one of the many links between modern pilgrims and their predecessors.

———

Like pilgrims, readers may benefit from a route map to give them an overview of the journey ahead: what follows is an outline of the various stages of this book. Its principal aim is to describe the course of Christian pilgrimage over the last two thousand years and place it in a historical context. Part of the fascination of the story of this pilgrimage tradition is that it has had its high and low points, comparable to the vicissitudes of an actual sacred journey. It evolved tentatively in the early centuries of Christianity, flourished in the Middle Ages, diminished after the Reformation, became diluted in the Age of Enlightenment, and revived in the nineteenth and twentieth centuries. But even at its lowest ebb, it has never disappeared.

The book's first two chapters set out some of the key questions about the nature of pilgrimage and explore possible pilgrimage traditions in the ancient world. Chapter One discusses the importance of the pilgrimage journey itself and investigates what makes a pilgrimage shrine different from other sacred places. It asks what makes a site holy, and whether *inner* transformation is central to the goal of the pilgrim. The second chapter investigates the possibility of sacred journeys in prehistoric societies and discusses "pilgrimages" in ancient classical times, including those to the healing sanctuary of Epidaurus and the oracle center of Delphi.

Chapters Three to Six describe the beginnings of the Christian cult of relics and saints, especially at Rome, and how the Holy Land became a key pilgrim destination during the reign of Emperor Constantine in the early fourth century. They relate how, in early medieval Europe (between the demise of the Roman Empire and the High Middle Ages), Christianity blossomed in Ireland, from where a stream of pilgrims, missionaries, and scholars flowed out to continental Europe; how pilgrimage was disrupted by the spread of Islam and the Viking incursions; and how conditions improved toward the end of the tenth century, when Europe became more peaceful and the church more vital and authoritative.

The next several chapters begin with the new millennium and the period of the Crusades from the late eleventh to the thirteenth century. By this time pilgrim shrines were established all around Europe, and pilgrimage was an accepted aspect of Christian life. This part of the book looks at some fundamental concepts associated with medieval pilgrimage, such as heaven, hell, purgatory, and indulgences; the importance of relics; and also the practicalities of making a journey to a shrine. It highlights key pilgrimage destinations. And it shows that by the later Middle Ages, the idea of pilgrimage was being challenged by religious critics and, in a more subtle way, by a nascent interest in travel and sightseeing. It describes how, after the Reformation, pilgrimage, especially in Protestant countries, declined dramatically, even ceased—or transmuted into quasi-pilgrimage activity such as the Grand Tour of the eighteenth century. Also discussed is the venerable place that pilgrimage holds in the Eastern Orthodox Church.

The last three chapters show how, in the nineteenth and twentieth centuries, pilgrimage was revitalized, perhaps because of a reaction to increasing industrialization and a need to supplement conventional forms of church worship with a more participatory approach. These chapters discuss the cult of the Virgin Mary and the rise of Marian shrines such as Lourdes, Knock, and Fátima; the revival of medieval sanctuaries such as Walsingham; and how Christian pilgrimage became a thriving phenomenon in parts of the New World, for example at the shrines of Our Lady of Guadalupe in Mexico City, Sainte-Anne-de-Beaupré near the city of Quebec, and Chimayo in New Mexico.

Finally, the Afterword recapitulates and reflects on the meaning, definition, and significance of pilgrimage. It discusses the present-day revival of the pilgrimage to Santiago de Compostela in Spain and the phenomenon of Taizé in France, the possibility of secular pilgrimage today, as well as the outlook for pilgrimage in the future.

1

WHAT IS PILGRIMAGE?

*"Whither will my path yet lead me? This path [. . .]
goes in spirals, perhaps in circles, but whichever
way it goes, I will follow it."*

Hermann Hesse, *Siddhartha*

For thousands of years the notion of pilgrimage has been inextricably associated with both a physical journey and an expression of
faith. If a religious person happened to live next door to a pilgrimage
shrine, such as Knock in Ireland, and visited it every so often, he or
she would probably not be thought of as a pilgrim. Equally, not every-
body who embarked on a long journey to a pilgrimage shrine would
necessarily be or become a pilgrim: atheists, skeptics, and agnostics
might happily travel to such sites as St. Peter's in Rome or the Church
of the Holy Sepulchre in Jerusalem and not feel a spiritual dimension
or want to be counted as pilgrims.

Journey and faith, then, are perhaps the starting points for a discussion about pilgrimage, especially now that journeys to shrines have
never been easier to accomplish. In medieval times, an English pilgrim
might have needed several months to travel from London to Rome.
Today it is possible to pray in Westminster Abbey at breakfast time

and gaze at Michelangelo's *Pietà* in St. Peter's the same afternoon. The ease with which people can travel to sacred sites has raised one of several questions about the essence of pilgrimage: how important is the nature of the journey to a shrine? If one person goes on a bus ride of a few hours to Fátima in Portugal and another walks there, taking several days, is there a sense in which the pilgrimage experience of the first person is not as fulfilling as that of the walker?

It would be tempting to equate the arduousness of a journey with the "merit" of a pilgrimage: the harder the trek, the more spiritually improving. Yet the answer must surely be that it depends on the emotional, mental, and spiritual state of the pilgrim. The person on the bus might have had a life crisis that brought on the urgent desire to visit Fátima. The walker, on the other hand, may simply have gone for the pleasure of a long hike and, while looking forward to arriving at the shrine, may feel tepid about its spiritual significance. So while the journey itself *is* central to pilgrimage, it may not matter how long, difficult, or dangerous it is, or if it is accomplished on foot or with a vehicle.

Another question: is it possible to be a pilgrim without going to a specific shrine or even making a physical journey at all? The words "pilgrim" and "pilgrimage" are derived from the Latin *peregrinus* (from *per*, "through," and *ager*, "field" or "land," so "pilgrimage" literally means "through the land"), which clearly suggests the idea of a journey and implies a predetermined destination. Yet there were Irish *peregrini*, i.e., pilgrims, in the early Middle Ages who left their country and set out "for the love of Christ" *without* a destination. They would get into boats without oars and let the wind, under the guidance of the Holy Spirit, blow them where it would. Were these men lesser pilgrims than those beating paths to well-known shrines?

Even if pilgrimage does not technically need a specific destination, it still implies a physical journey, as well as an accompanying state of serious inner reflection—which some would term "religious" or "spiritual"—to distinguish it from mere travel or sightseeing. Yet consider the fifteenth-century mystic Thomas à Kempis, who said that no matter where a person was, he or she would always be a "stranger and pilgrim," unable to find peace unless united inwardly with Christ: for him, true pilgrimage was not slogging along a track to a shrine but an inner journey along the pathway of the spirit, with the living Christ as the ultimate shrine. The English Puritan John Bunyan's great allegorical work *The Pilgrim's Progress* (1678) also presented pilgrimage as an inner journey, one designed to overcome moral obstacles and gain self-knowledge in order to arrive at the Celestial City. Its readers become pilgrims in the imagination, accompanying the character of Christian as he walks through the Valley of Humiliation, resists the temptations of Vanity Fair, or escapes from Doubting-Castle.

Pilgrimage, then, may refer to an inner—emotional, mental, and spiritual—journey as well as an outer, physical one: for Kempis and Bunyan it is possible for the pilgrim to remain in a cloister or a prison cell and yet go on a pilgrimage. Even so, inner pilgrimage, like its external counterpart, still implies *movement*—toward a new spiritual state of being. Therefore, whether pilgrimage is made physically or contemplatively, the idea of journeying remains central to it: the pilgrim must make a journey because he or she needs time—time to reflect on personal milestones or conflicts, or upon the great mysteries of life such as love, fate, suffering, and the nature of God. For the pilgrim, the journey, with all its vicissitudes, is not the wearisome preamble to truth—it is the necessary way to truth, the living, arduous, and joyful process by which truth can be attained.

Pilgrimage has inherent challenges, whether embarked on inwardly or outwardly. It is a journey not to be taken lightly: the physical challenges of heat, cold, rain, pain, and fatigue—and likewise interior hardships—can open up the mind to old memories and new possibilities as well as effect an emotional and spiritual purification.

What is essential is that the journey, by whatever means it is accomplished, gives the pilgrim enough time to expose himself or herself to the possibility of a sacred metamorphosis. If that is done, the destination—a shrine, a holy mountain, or a house of God—will signify not the end of the journey, but the start: a gateway into a new way of being, of seeing life afresh with spiritually cleansed eyes.

Apart from the likes of the medieval Irish *peregrini*, pilgrims have always needed a sacred destination, a shrine, for their journey, and this begs the question, what makes a shrine a pilgrimage place as opposed to any holy sanctuary?

Every religious tradition has its shrines, buildings, objects, or natural features deemed holy for one reason or another. One widespread factor that determines a place's sacredness is its association with a holy person or mystic, or apparitions and other miracles that reportedly occurred there.

In Mexico City, for example, there are many churches, not least the imposing Metropolitan Cathedral. Yet pilgrims flock in huge numbers to one of these churches, the Basilica of Our Lady of Guadalupe, because it holds what is said to be a "miraculously created" image of the Virgin Mary, an image that may work a transformation in a visitor. Perhaps that is the key to a pilgrimage place: the notion of transformation, spiritual and bodily. One of the main reasons pilgrims have journeyed to pilgrim shrines has been the hope that they will be cured of a specific illness or ailment or shifted from a mental or emotional rut. (In Christianity, the agent of transformation has traditionally been the power of a saint, as transmitted through his or her relics.) By making contact with, or getting near to and venerating, a shrine's holy object, pilgrims believe or hope they will be transformed in a positive way. This is the reason ancient Greek "pilgrims" went to the healing shrine of Epidaurus—to find a cure for ailments ranging from rheumatism to blindness. It is also why pilgrims went to the myriad shrines of medieval Europe, and why seekers today go to modern sanctuaries associated with transformative healing.

Of course, outwardly it is often impossible nowadays to distinguish a pilgrim from a walker or tourist, and categories such as "pilgrim" and "traveler" are fluid. The membrane between the sacred and the secular is porous. Tourists might harbor "pilgrim feelings," and pilgrims might have "tourist interests." In the final analysis only the pilgrim knows whether he or she is on a pilgrimage as opposed to, say, a vacation. And even then, that sense of being a pilgrim might shift in terms of conviction during the journey.

In summary, the traditional spiritual pilgrimage usually involves a physical journey (which may or may not be long and arduous) to a special destination, accompanied by a particular state of mind and often with the hope of transformation. But it is not absolutely necessary to go on a pilgrimage with the single-minded aim of being transformed. Some pilgrims have gone, and still go, to shrines simply to thank God or a saint for being saved from a disaster or critical situation; theirs is a pilgrimage based on gratitude or celebration or fulfilling a vow rather than the need for transformation. Others may make pilgrimages for other reasons, such as breaking out of their daily routines; or they may go without a clearly defined intention in mind—it may be an impulse, a longing that requires no justification or reasoning at all.

———

This book tells the story of pilgrimage in the Western world and its rise, peak, decline, and revival. The first Christian pilgrimage journey could be said to be the journey of the Magi to the Christ child. But Christian writers have also looked back to the Hebrew Bible to find inspiration for the idea of pilgrimage, one example being Abraham, who was called upon by God to leave his home and to start a new life in the land of Canaan. Abraham's summons is the archetypal call of the pilgrim—the irresistible prompting to exchange the familiar with the strange, the secure with the unknown, a life of ongoing domesticity with one charged with divine meaning. The exodus of the Children of Israel from bondage in Egypt and their trek through the wilderness, led by Moses, has also provided a paradigm for Christians: a journey of danger and hardship, of backsliding and miraculous help, and an arrival in the home promised by God—again, Canaan.

Christianity holds that the "promised land" is, ultimately, heaven, and life is often viewed as a pilgrimage of the soul to this divine place or state. St. Paul, in his Second Letter to the Corinthians (5:1–17), said that for as long as we are alive on earth we are conscious of being absent from God, and that "we groan, longing to be clothed with our heavenly dwelling." The Letter to the Hebrews (11:13–16) refers to people being "strangers" and "pilgrims" on earth, longing for a "heavenly" country. And St. Augustine of Hippo wrote that people were like "travelers" moving away from God and that to return to the true homeland—heaven—we must "use this world, not enjoy it."

For Christians, therefore, in addition to the traditional reasons for making pilgrimage mentioned above—and experiencing *communitas*, or fellowship, with other pilgrims—pilgrimage has a deep symbolic resonance. Making a journey to a sacred center represents the journey of the soul through the travails of mortal life to heaven. It is perhaps this powerful sense of a divine destiny, of an ultimate heavenly destination, that has given Christian pilgrimage its depth and broad appeal, enabling it to endure for two millennia, with no signs of abating.

For every pilgrim making a physical journey, the sore feet, enforced detours, and anxieties, as well as the companionship and acts of generous hospitality, represent in microcosm the woes and weals of life. The pilgrim's final arrival at the shrine, the source of holiness, signifies the soul's entering a state of blessedness, a rehearsal on earth for what heaven has in store. Of course, for the pilgrim—unlike the immortal soul—there is the question of returning, a process of disengaging from the sanctified place and state, from temporary oneness with the divine, and of reintegration with the secular, the familiar world of "home." Yet for those pilgrims who have successfully committed themselves in thought and action to the transformatory journey, their adjustment to the quotidian will be sustained by a fresh attitude toward it, by the knowledge that they have reenacted the journey of the soul and glimpsed the blessed state, even if only in a fragmentary way.

2

SACRED JOURNEYS
IN ANCIENT TIMES

"Blind in one eye, Ambrosia of Athens came as a
suppliant to the god Asclepius."

Inscription from the healing shrine
of Asclepius at Epidaurus

If people did not have a spiritual or religious capacity, the pilgrimage tradition would never have begun; and this belief in a supernatural dimension, as well as the desire to perform rituals to gain divine favor, is probably as old as humankind itself. There is enough evidence to suggest that our prehistoric ancestors performed religious rituals. But did they go on "pilgrimage"? Certainly in historical times, when written records were first made, there is material evidence (such as scriptures, artifacts, and the remains of temples and tombs) to indicate that people all over the world, from the ancient Greeks, Romans, and Celts in the West, to the Indians and Chinese in the East, practiced religious rituals that included sacred journeys.

The evidence for such journeys in prehistoric times—before, say, the fourth millennium BCE—is less easy to judge. For example, was the great megalithic circle of Stonehenge in England a temple, a tribal meeting place, or a site that combined a number of different functions? Was it a sacred destination? Without written evidence it is difficult to surmise.

If prehistoric cultures had recognizable sacred centers, it opens up the possibility that people made journeys to such centers, beyond visits of normal everyday worship—meaning, they may have made "pilgrimages."

During the time of the Upper Paleolithic ("Old Stone Age") Period, from about 40,000 to 10,000 BCE, "modern" human beings (*Homo sapiens*) were creating cave paintings, for example at Lascaux in France and Altamira in Spain, which may have had a magical or religious function, such as invoking divine help for hunting the bison, deer, and other animals portrayed in their murals. (Artists of this period were also creating carved sculptures of female figures, such as the so-called Venus of Willendorf in Austria.) It is not impossible that richly decorated caves such as Lascaux were sacred destinations, though their size and relative inaccessibility would probably have precluded any large-scale assemblies.

In the Neolithic ("New Stone Age") Period, beginning in about 10,000 BCE, people gradually turned from hunting and gathering to growing crops, domesticating animals, and developing crafts, such as pottery and weaving. Perhaps their most visually impressive achievements were their megalithic monuments. These ancient stone structures still haunt the landscapes of many parts of Europe, especially along the Atlantic coast. They were built mainly during the fourth and third millennia BCE and range from single standing stones, or menhirs, to grand stone arrangements and tombs.

The most spectacular alignment of standing stones in Europe can be found at Carnac in Brittany, where more than 3,000 upright stones are aligned in three principal groups, their parallel rows making them look like soldiers on parade. What function the stones had is a mystery; suggestions include that they marked burial plots or had an astronomical and therefore calendrical purpose, or served to demarcate a processional way. The labor involved in erecting them must have been immense—and the spectacle of these stone regiments must have conferred prestige on the immediate community and perhaps drawn visitors. But as to how "sacred" the stones were and whether there was anything like "pilgrimages" to them is unknown.

One of the finest examples of a passage tomb is Newgrange, which lies beside the River Boyne in County Meath in Ireland. It forms part of a complex of monuments that includes the mounds of Dowth and Knowth, along with a number of smaller tombs. Newgrange itself, which dates to about the late fourth millennium BCE, has a gently curving dome that measures about 40 feet high and 250 feet in diameter. It conceals a 20-foot-high domed chamber, the entrance to which is via a 60-foot-long tunnel-like passageway.

What has provoked attention among scholars is the fact that Newgrange is aligned with the sunrise on the day of the winter solstice, when sunbeams move along the passage into the chamber and illuminate its interior. It is easy to imagine that this moment would have had a profound religious significance for the community that built Newgrange, inaugurating the lengthening of days. It is also plausible that there were rituals associated with the winter solstice. And perhaps there were "pilgrimages" made to Newgrange by members of outlying communities, wishing to participate in the communal sense of renewal and reborn light.

Like Carnac's avenues of menhirs and the great tombs, Neolithic stone circles were probably the focus for a community, though it is not clear what function they had. It is possible they were assembly points for rituals or festivals. That the stones were often aligned with the sun and the moon at certain times of the year (such as those of Stonehenge with the summer solstice) suggests they were used as calendars of some sort.

One of the largest stone circles in the world is at Avebury in England; it is part of the same prehistoric landscape as Stonehenge (which lies about eighteen miles to the south). Constructed in the third millennium BCE, Avebury comprises a huge "henge" (a circular earth bank and ditch), within which is a large circle of standing stones. This stone circle surrounds another two smaller stone circles.

The function of Avebury is unknown, but the scale of the site must have made it famous and a possible draw for visitors.

Stonehenge was built over a period of about a thousand years. Its henge was created in about 3100 BCE, but it was not until around 2500 BCE that its huge Sarsen stones and smaller so-called bluestones were set up. As with Carnac, Stonehenge's purpose has been keenly debated. The alignment of stones suggests an astronomical function, and they also form part of an area that contains a large number of pre-historic mounds. Perhaps Stonehenge was multifunctional, serving as a temple, a celestial observatory, and a place where religious rituals and festivals could be staged?

In summary, it is impossible to be certain what happened at Neolithic sites such as Carnac, Newgrange, Avebury, and Stonehenge. But it can be said that an enormous deal of time, labor, and craft were expended on each of them. Carnac's stones, some of which rise more than twelve feet high, were carefully placed in customized pits to keep them stable. Stonehenge's bluestones were brought all the way from the Preseli Hills in Wales, about 150 miles away, on sledges and rafts by land and sea. And some of Newgrange's stones have carvings with various intricate and enigmatic patterns. These monuments must have been great achievements for their respective communities, and it is difficult not to believe they had a religious function—which, in turn, opens up the possibility that they also served as sacred destinations for visitors from farther away.

———

If our prehistoric ancestors built monuments for religious rituals, it is likely they also revered, and perhaps made "pilgrimages" to, particular nature sites such as mountains, islands, and water locations, which have traditionally been regarded as abodes of the gods or spirits in various religions all over the world.

For the ancient Greeks, Mount Olympus (popularly identified with the Olympus massif south of Thessaloniki) was the seat of Zeus and his immortal family, and Mount Parnassus in the center of the country was sacred to Apollo and reputed to be the home of the Muses. For the Romans, the mountain now called Monte Cavo in the Alban Hills near Rome was the site of a temple dedicated to Jupiter.

Mountains also loom large as sacred places in the Bible. Moses encountered God on Mount Sinai, and Jesus's transfiguration took place on a mountain. Although the church was to become hostile toward nature sites originally associated with pagan gods, Christian mountain pilgrimages take place to this day, for example on Croagh Patrick in Ireland. In other religions, mountains such as Mount Kailas in Tibet, sacred to Hindus, Buddhists, and Jains, and Mount Fuji, one of Japan's holiest mountains, have attracted pilgrims for many centuries.

Another enduring aspect of nature considered to be sacred is water, traditionally recognized as an agent of spiritual purification and of healing: lakes, rivers, waterfalls, and springs around the world have been the goal of pilgrims for thousands of years. In the West, there has always been a strong pilgrimage tradition centered on holy springs and wells, many of them dedicated to Christian saints, but with origins going back to pagan times. In Ireland, the tradition of going to wells for healing still continues, with many pilgrims leaving offerings and sometimes tying strips of clothing or rags to a tree (usually a whitethorn) next to the well.

––––––

With the dawn of history, that is to say written records, the evidence for sacred journeys in ancient Europe gains a whole new dimension, with accounts by classical authors supplementing archaeological findings. "Pilgrimage" was found not only in ancient Greece and Rome but also Egypt and Phoenicia. The Greek historian Herodotus (in the fifth century BCE), for example, described what appears to be a regular Egyptian spiritual journey to the town of Boubastis, home of the goddess Bastet-Artemis, in the Nile Delta. Herodotus said that travelers of both sexes sailed down the Nile, in various crafts, the joyous atmosphere being whipped up by singing, clapping, and flute playing. The boats would stop at various towns along the way, with the female pilgrims performing traditional rituals at each place, until they reached Boubastis. There they would join in the festivities and sacrifices, "and more wine of grapes is consumed upon that festival than during the whole of the rest of the year." Herodotus claimed seven hundred thousand travelers would gather at Boubastis every year, a figure that is probably exaggerated but which indicates a sizable crowd journeyed there.

In ancient Phoenicia, sacred travel took place in conjunction with the cult of the god Adonis (from Canaanite *Adon*, meaning "lord") in and around the city of Byblos, the ruins of which lie about twenty miles north of Beirut. In legend, the handsome young Adonis was loved by Astarte, the Near Eastern goddess who became assimilated with Aphrodite (Greek) and Venus (Roman). One time, while hunting on the mountain, Adonis was gored by a wild boar and died. His blood flowed into the nearby river and turned it red. He descended to the underworld where he was held by the goddess Proserpine (Persephone). Eventually, Astarte successfully pleaded for his release, and Adonis returned to the upper world.

Byblos was a substantial city, and its festival of Adonis would have drawn "pilgrims" from afar. It was also a noisy one. The second-century CE writer Lucian of Samosata related that women "beat their breasts and wail every year, and perform their secret ritual amid signs of mourning through the whole countryside. When they have finished their mourning and wailing, they sacrifice in the first place to Adonis, as to one who has departed this life: after this they allege that he is alive again, and exhibit his effigy to the sky."

The worship of Adonis was not confined to the city of Byblos. The valley of the Adonis River (modern Nahr Ibrahim), just east of Byblos, was also sacred to the god, and an annual journey was made to his temple erected at the source of the river, high up on a boar-haunted crag. The river itself, which, owing to the presence of iron ore has a ruddy color after the annual spring thaw, may have suggested itself as an appropriate location for the death of Adonis and the spilling of his blood.

———

In ancient Greece, by about the eighth or seventh century BCE, Pan-hellenic festivals were being held on a four-year cycle at Olympia and

Delphi, and in two-year intervals at Corinth and Nemea. They combined religious rituals, including sacrifices, with sporting events and productions of plays. Before a festival took place, a "sacred truce" was announced throughout Greece to allow participants to travel without hindrance. Each festival honored a particular god—Olympia and Nemea were both dedicated to Zeus—and visitors partook in the ritual sacrifice of an animal and brought votive offerings, such as jewelry and metal tripods (used as seats or as stands for offerings). They also purchased statuettes of divine figures as religious souvenirs, just as modern Christians might do at Rome, Lourdes, or Fátima.

Although most visitors to these festivals were there to compete in the games or engage in diplomacy or trade, there would have been many for whom the religious cult and rituals were of great significance—and who might therefore be considered as "pilgrims."

As well as Panhellenic festivals, there were also shrines that drew visitors from across Greece. Some, such as Eleusis near Athens, were famed for their mystery cults (spiritual societies with secret initiation rituals), while others were known for their oracles or as healing sanctuaries. The most famous oracle was at Delphi, in the center of the country, though those at Dodona and Didyma were important, too. At Delphi a priestess known as the Pythia would be consulted by visitors on matters of everyday life, such as business ventures or marriage. Their questions were written down on tablets and handed to the Pythia by a priest. The Pythia would then apparently enter a trance and be inspired by the god Apollo to pour forth a stream of words that only the priest could interpret. He would write down his "translation" and hand it back to the questioner. The Delphic oracle was notorious for its ambivalent replies. Yet the fact that the oracle lasted for so long (until the end of the fourth century CE) suggests it was trusted for its advice.

Other prophetic women in the Greek world were the sibyls, the most famous one of whom was associated with the oracular shrine of Cumae near Naples. Individual visitors may have come to consult her, but the evidence is lacking. The Sibylline Books were a collection of oracular utterances said to have been spoken by a sibyl and preserved in a number of volumes. Although their creation is shrouded in mystery, they eventually came into the possession of the Roman government and were used for guidance at times of national crisis.

Healing shrines were also popular destinations in the classical world, for example on the Greek island of Kos, but particularly at Epidaurus in the Peloponnese. The god Asclepius presided over these and other healing sanctuaries, called asclepeions. Spiritual seekers would typically travel there to undergo what was called an incubation. This involved spending the night within the sacred enclosure to await a dream in which Asclepius would appear and indicate, or even effect, a cure for the visitors' ailments. If the incubation was successful, they would leave behind an inscribed tablet thanking the god. Many of these tablets have survived, including two from Epidaurus that can be dated to the mid-fourth century BCE. The first of these was dedicated by a blind man named Alcetas of Helieis, who dreamed that the god opened his blind eyes with his fingers; Alcetas reported waking up in the morning and seeing the trees in the sanctuary compound for the first time. Another Epidaurus tablet described the visit of a half-blind woman named Ambrosia of Athens, who was skeptical of some of the cures: "But when she slept in the shrine the god stood over her and seemed to say he would cure her as long as she gave to the temple a silver pig as a memorial of her unbelief. Saying this, he cut open her diseased eye and poured in a potion. When morning came she went away cured."

Although it is clear that travelers in the classical world trod the roads, tracks, and paths that led to sacred centers, scholars still debate to what extent they can be called "pilgrims" in a way that Christians and those of other world religions would recognize. One significant factor is that the Greeks did not have a word for "pilgrim" in our sense of the word. One term they used was *theoros*, which means "he who sees the vision" and referred to an official delegate sent by a city-state to a festival or an oracle. If, as Matthew Dillon has written, pilgrimage is "a religious activity which involves travel away from home, a break from normal affairs, and a time away from domestic duties," then

Greek *theoroi* and individuals going to shrines and oracles could be counted as "pilgrims."

But as Scott Scullion has pointed out, Greek *theoroi* did not seem to consider the *journey* to a shrine as being sacred, and we may heed Scullion's warning not to apply the term "pilgrim" unthinkingly to various classical travelers, "as though all those attending a panhellenic festival considered themselves pilgrims on a sacred mission."

In the end we can only guess to what extent ancient travelers to shrines such as Boubastis, Byblos, Epidaurus, or Delphi shared something of the same mentality of Christian pilgrims, namely faith, hope, and the desire for transformation, albeit within a different supernatural mindset.

3

EARLY PATHS

"We took his [St. Polycarp's] bones, counting them more precious than the most exquisite gems and more pure than gold . . ."

The congregants of Smyrna

The first pilgrims associated with the Christian faith were arguably the Magi, the "three wise men," who, according to the Gospel of Matthew, journeyed from the east to Bethlehem, guided by a star, to visit the infant Jesus. Their story contains some of the classic elements of pilgrimage. First and foremost there was a journey. In their case this would have probably been a long one from Persia, since, according to Herodotus, "Magi" was in fact the name of the priestly caste of the Medes, a people who lived within the Persian Empire and were renowned as soothsayers and astrologers. Like pilgrims before and after them, the Magi who sought out Jesus were anxious to experience and honor a source—for Christians *the* source—of sacred awe. Also, in line with the long and continuous pilgrim tradition of leaving an offering behind at a sanctuary, they paid reverence in the form of gifts: gold, incense, and myrrh. For later Christians these gifts came to symbolize royalty, divinity (incense was burned during religious ceremonies), and Jesus's passion (myrrh was used to embalm corpses).

What distinguishes the Magi's alleged journey from most other later Christian pilgrimages was that they came to see a *living being*, not the relics of someone who had died. But their longing was the same, namely the desire for contact with a source of holiness. This was usually the first prerequisite for Christian pilgrimage; and it commonly took the form of the bones or other material remains of a martyr or saint. The rationale for this was that the godliness exhibited by certain individuals during their lives could be transmitted through their relics and be of benefit to those who came to see and touch them. This idea in turn presupposed that inanimate objects could generate or transmit divine power. Glimpses of this belief can be seen in the New Testament. In Matthew 9:20–22 a woman suffering from a blood disorder came up behind Jesus and touched his clothing, thinking to herself, "If I only touch his cloak, I will be healed," and so she was. In the Acts of the Apostles 19:11–12 it is said that while St. Paul was residing in Ephesus in Asia Minor, "God did extraordinary miracles" through him, so that "even handkerchiefs and aprons that had touched him were taken to the sick, and their illnesses were cured and the evil spirits left them."

The cult of holy relics lay, and still lies, at the heart of pilgrimage; but it is not entirely clear whether the faithful believed that spiritual energy was stored in these sacred objects or whether they were simply the means through which the power of God could flow, like a magnifying glass intensifying the rays of the sun. The fourth-century churchman St. Cyril of Jerusalem, for instance, thought that relics were repositories of actual spiritual virtue and cited the incident in the Hebrew Bible when the corpse of a man, accidentally put into the tomb of Elisha, sprang back to life on touching the prophet's bones. Later, in the Middle Ages, St. Thomas Aquinas took a different view, saying that God honored relics by working miracles in their presence—that is, the relics were the channel for cures and miracles, but did not directly cause them themselves.

If relics or other sources of spiritual benefit were indispensable to pilgrimage, another crucial factor was a place where they could be accessed. It might be possible to obtain a cure from a living saint, but if he or she were moving about all the time, it made pilgrimage difficult. The idea of pilgrimage implied a fixed destination, such as a tomb, a church, or a grotto, and this place often came to be venerated as much as the relics it held, since it was believed the surroundings could absorb the relics' divine energy.

In the early centuries of the church, the faithful began to visit the tombs of those who had been renowned for their saintliness, or for their inspirational display of fortitude while being persecuted or put to death. The tradition of Christian martyrs—those willing to die for the sake of Christ—began with Stephen, who, according to Acts 6:8–7:60, was stoned to death after his fierce denunciation of the Jewish faith. The constant oppression of Christians within the Roman Empire, from Emperor Nero (r. 54–68 CE) to the great persecution that occurred during the reign of Diocletian (r. 284–305 CE), added an increasing number of martyrs to the ranks of the blessed. In fact the Romans were on the whole tolerant of other people's beliefs, but they generally considered Christians to be obdurate "atheists" (i.e., they did not recognize the Roman gods) and made them convenient scapegoats for disasters, whether natural or manmade. The Church Father Tertullian remarked that "if the Tiber rises too high or the Nile sinks too low, the cry is 'The Christians to the lion!'" But he also noted that the blood of the martyrs was the seed of the church: every Christian put to death meant another opportunity for establishing a cult and strengthening the corporate unity of the living and the dead within the church.

A classic example of how the relics of a martyr came to be venerated can be seen in the case of the second-century bishop St. Polycarp of Smyrna in Asia Minor. His death is described in a circular letter written by members of his congregation, who tell how their bishop, well advanced in age, was hunted down by the Roman authorities and taken off to the local arena and execution ground. Inside, Polycarp was given the chance to save his life by swearing allegiance to Caesar and proclaiming, "Away with the atheists [i.e., Christians]!" Polycarp did shout out the phrase, but as he did so he provocatively gestured toward the ranks of baying pagans. He was then told to reject Christ, but he replied, famously, "For eighty-six years I have served him, and he never did me any harm: how can I now blaspheme my King and Savior?" Unable to break his faith or spirit, the Romans sentenced him to death by burning. But when the fire began to rage around him it suddenly took a shape "like the sail of a ship when filled by wind" and formed a circle around the bishop, making him shine like "gold and silver glowing in a furnace." He was then stabbed and his body placed in the flames. Afterward, the Smyrna Christians gathered his bones and placed them "in a suitable place, where with joy and good cheer we shall congregate, as opportunity lets us, and the Lord shall grant us to celebrate the anniversary of his martyrdom."

In addition to mentioning two important ingredients of pilgrimage—bones "more precious than [. . .] gems" and "a suitable place" to keep them—the story of Polycarp also refers to a third component: a devoted group of believers ready to gather at the shrine in celebration. An idea of how the cult of martyrs evolved further is suggested by the fourth-century saint Gregory of Nyssa. In his speech about the martyr Theodore of Amasea, a Roman soldier who was said to have been executed in 306 for refusing to relinquish his Christian faith, Gregory alludes to an "ornate structure" that had been built over the martyr's remains and also to the fact that even dust from the tomb was a "gift and treasure." Gregory also said that St. Theodore "attends on God," to whom he can pass on the prayers of petitioners. This was a belief that would sustain pilgrims and other faithful through the centuries: the saint or martyr was thought of as a friend who could intercede on behalf of the petitioner. From this it was a short step to believing that being buried near a saint would increase one's chances of being received into the company of saints and the presence of God on the Day of Judgment.

This idea—that proximity to a saint could help you in the afterlife—in turn led Christians to put greater emphasis on their burial rituals and their cemeteries, where, during the fourth and fifth centuries, it became the practice to build elaborate tombs and to hold public worship. One late-fourth-century Christian inscription from Rome states that the deceased had got a tomb near the threshold of saints—something, it says, "many desire but few receive." So the tomb of the saint became the focus for burials, for local worship, and, on anniversaries, for large gatherings of the faithful—the first regular groups of Christian pilgrims. Gregory of Nyssa described the crowds flocking to St. Theodore's tomb to celebrate his annual festival, and depicted the road to his tomb teeming with people "like ants, some coming and others leaving."

———

In the early Christian era, the most frequented pilgrimage places were found in Rome, where Christians buried their dead in labyrinthine underground passages and chambers known as catacombs. There were also catacombs in Naples, Sicily, and Malta, but Rome's were the most famous and extensive. The Roman catacombs were carved out of the tufa (soft porous rock) mainly around the roads that fanned out from the city. Bodies of the faithful were covered in lime, wrapped in cloth, and placed in rectangular niches known as *loculi*, chipped out of the sides of the passages. There were also *cubicula*, or tomb chambers, for more prestigious burials or for the dead of more than one family. Christians created these underground tombs because burial was forbidden inside Rome's walls (pagan Romans usually practiced cremation and deposited the ashes of their loved ones in urns). Professional Christian diggers known as *fossores* were responsible for creating the catacomb cemeteries, many of which lay on land given by wealthy individuals. If space was limited, the *fossores* would dig out galleries on different levels—sometimes up to four or five.

About forty second-century catacombs have been unearthed in Rome. Something of the atmosphere that early pilgrims experienced when visiting these tombs can be gleaned from a description given by St. Jerome, who lived in Rome as a boy in the mid-fourth century. Jerome used to go to the catacombs on Sundays to visit the "tombs of apostles and martyrs." The descent into the ground, the darkness, and the recesses in the walls filled with corpses brought to his mind the words of Psalm 55:15, "Let them go down into hell alive." Every so often the darkness was partially dispelled by light let in through chimney-like shafts called *luminaria*. Then, as Jerome moved away from the light, the darkness quickly enclosed him again, reminding him of the scene in Virgil's *Aeneid* in which the hero, Aeneas, searches for his wife Creüsa at night while the Greeks sack Troy—"everywhere a sense of dread afflicted me, as did the very silence itself."

But it would be wrong to suppose that the catacombs were merely dark, creepy places. The *cubicula* resembled small chapels and were places of warmth and welcome, gaily painted with life-affirming scenes from the Bible expressing, for instance, belief in the resurrection through depictions of Christ raising Lazarus from the dead, or proclaiming the ideal of Christian fellowship with murals showing people eating and drinking together at funeral banquets or eucharistic meals. Visitors came to pay their respects or to pray at the tombs of their relatives and friends (who, according to the inscriptions and emblems, included doctors, carpenters, smiths, and bakers), or they came to celebrate the anniversaries of the martyrs with wine, bread, and the singing of hymns. (The remains of glass drinking vessels have been found there, decorated with gold-leaf pictures of saints and biblical scenes.)

The numbers of pilgrims coming to the Roman catacombs increased during the fourth century, when the *luminaria* were first constructed to add light and improve the air supply, and stairways were widened to improve access. The dynamic reciprocal relationship between the living and the dead can be inferred from tomb inscriptions and graffiti left by visitors. An inscription on the tomb of a woman named Agape asks pilgrims to "remember your dear Agape so that Almighty God may keep her in eternity"—an often-found plea that later theologians took as evidence of belief in purgatory. If the dead requested prayers from the living, the living requested intercession from the dead, as numerous graffiti show, for example in the catacombs of Calepodius and Callistus.

Perhaps the most interesting of the pilgrims' graffiti are in the catacomb of St. Sebastian on the Via Appia, where the apostles St. Peter and St. Paul were venerated. Several hundred graffiti are addressed to them, most with simple invocations such as "Peter and Paul, help Primitivus a sinner" or "Paul and Peter, pray for Victor."

By the end of the fourth century, the Roman poet Prudentius was able to describe the crowds of pilgrims flocking to the tomb of the martyr St. Hippolytus and to refer to the "countless martyrs' tombs" in Rome. But as the Eternal City became prey to various Germanic peoples in the fifth and sixth centuries, the catacombs, unprotected by the city walls, grew less attractive as burial sites and pilgrim destinations, and gradually fell into decay. The Goths plundered them in 537, and the Lombards did the same in 756. Two years later, Pope Paul I began to transfer the sacred bones of martyrs into the city, a process continued by his immediate successors. Within a few centuries the catacombs were virtually forgotten and remained so until the sixteenth century, when the Italian antiquarian Antonio Bosio—the "Columbus of the Catacombs"—began exploring them.

4

THE AGE OF
CONSTANTINE

"Moreover, in visiting the holy places, so great was the passion and the enthusiasm she [Paula] exhibited for each, that she could never have torn herself away from one had she not been eager to visit the rest."

St. Jerome, describing a pilgrimage
to the Holy Land

In the year 312, the fortunes of the church changed radically and permanently when, in a struggle to become emperor, the Roman general Constantine defeated his rival, Maxentius, in a battle in which he was apparently inspired by a vision of the cross in the sky. Now, as emperor of the Western Roman Empire (and later also the Eastern Empire), Constantine proceeded to make Christianity the most favored religion in his dominions. Every succeeding Roman emperor but one was Christian, at least in name, and the bishops of Rome became increasingly influential in both the spiritual and the political spheres.

Although there are doubts about Constantine's exclusive devotion to Christianity, he took measures to elevate the status of the faith:

the church was allowed the legal right to inherit property, clergy were exempt from taxation and service in public office, clerical celibacy was no longer subject to fiscal penalties, Sunday was made a public holiday, and state funds were made available for church use. Constantine himself took a keen interest in church affairs and presided at the Council of Nicaea in 325, at which the Arian heresy (the doctrine that held that Jesus Christ was not truly divine) was condemned. He endowed the church with property from all over the empire, including Rome itself, where he built the Church of St. Peter on Vatican Hill. He also made the ancient Greek city of Byzantium in Asia Minor his capital, renaming it Constantinople.

From the time of Constantine onward, the Holy Land became an increasingly popular destination for pilgrims hoping they could draw nearer to God through contact with the actual places touched by Christ. Fourth-century graffiti on the walls of churches in Nazareth and Capernaum indicate that visitors came from many different parts of the empire. This surge of pilgrim activity owed much to the efforts of Constantine's mother, Helena, a fervent Christian who, in 326 (when she was in her seventies), set off to visit the Holy Land. In Jerusalem she allegedly excavated Jesus's tomb and discovered the cross on which he had been crucified. Soon bits of this so-called True Cross were circulating all over Christendom—Cyril of Jerusalem remarked that "The whole world is filled with [them]." St. Paulinus of Nola, for example, had a splinter that was *in segmento pene atomo*—"almost as small as an atom."

With the enthusiasm and material support of Constantine and Helena, grand Christian churches began to rise in Palestine. Jerusalem itself now had monumental shrines befitting its central position in the Christian faith. The most important of these was the Church of the Holy Sepulchre, built on what was believed to be the site of Jesus's execution and his burial nearby. One of the most resonant shrines for Christian pilgrims to this day, the church was originally a complex of buildings that featured a circular, domed structure known as the Anastasis ("Resurrection"); next to it was the Martyrion, a large, richly carved and gilded basilica designed for large congregations. The church was twice destroyed and restored during succeeding centuries until, in the 1140s, the Crusaders amalgamated the different buildings under one roof—the layout that it still has today.

Perhaps one of the first travelers to witness Constantine's building program was the anonymous Bordeaux Pilgrim, who in 333–34 made the earliest recorded pilgrimage from western Europe to the Holy Land. Unfortunately, the account he—or possibly she—left is mostly an unembellished list of the stages of the journey, which, if a little monotonous, at least shows the impressive imperial network of roads and hostels. From Bordeaux in southwest France this pilgrim made his way eastward to Toulouse and Valence before crossing the Alps into Italy. From there he traveled through the Balkans to Constantinople, then rode south through what is now Turkey and Syria to Jerusalem. (He claimed to have covered 3,250 miles, made 190 stops, and changed horses 360 times.)

In Jerusalem, the pilgrim mentions a number of sights, including the recently built Church of the Holy Sepulchre, "of wondrous beauty," along with its external water tanks and "bath" for baptizing infants. His guides also showed him, perhaps more controversially, the very palm tree whose branches were used to strew the path of Jesus as he made his entry into Jerusalem, and the column against which Jesus was scourged. The pilgrim also visited the nearby village of Bethany, where Jesus was said to have raised Lazarus from the dead, the ruins of the ancient city of Jericho, and the Dead Sea—a curiosity for pilgrims down the ages—whose water was "very bitter" and without fish, and "if anyone dives in for a swim, the water turns him over."

Other evidence for the popularity of the Holy Land as a destination for pilgrims during the fourth and fifth centuries can be found in the writings of St. Jerome (c. 347–419/420) and the account of a pilgrim named Egeria (also known as Etheria and Sylvia), probably a nun from Spain or southern France who traveled to the Levant in the early 380s. Although much of Egeria's account has been lost, it is more engaging and informative than that of the Bordeaux Pilgrim. Egeria is constantly enthusiastic about what she does and sees, and she makes careful note of anything relevant to her faith or of practical value to her fellow nuns back home. She mentions, for example, that during Lent the Jerusalem Christians did not eat oil or anything that grows on trees, "but only water and a little gruel made from flour." She also gives tantalizing glimpses of places outside Palestine, such as Constantinople and Edessa.

In Jerusalem itself Egeria paid close attention to the order and content of church services and left an invaluable guide to late-fourth-century Christian liturgy. She describes the Sunday services at the Church of the Holy Sepulchre, where people gathered in great numbers outside the basilica before dawn, singing hymns and antiphons. At the first cockcrow the bishop arrived and the congregation proceeded to the Anastasis, where psalms and prayers were recited and censers brought in, filling the interior with fragrance. The bishop then read the narrative of Jesus's resurrection from the New Testament, eliciting weeping and groaning from the congregation. Elsewhere she describes the veneration of the True Cross on Good Friday. The bishop took the sacred wood out of its silver-gilt casket and held it firmly at either end while members of the congregation came up one by one to kiss it—Egeria mentions that a number of deacons stood around the bishop to guard the wood because someone had once tried to bite off a piece of it.

A few years after Egeria's pilgrimage, St. Jerome, best known for his translation of the Bible into Latin (the Vulgate), came to Palestine and settled in Bethlehem for the remainder of his life. Through his authority, writings, and enthusiasm both for the Holy Land and for the cult of the martyrs, Jerome was influential in helping to consolidate the positive attitude of contemporary and later Christians toward the veneration of relics and pilgrimages to sacred places. Jerome was born in Stridon (Dalmatia) and educated at home and in Rome, where, as mentioned, he visited the catacombs. In about 374 he set off to the East and stayed for a while in Antioch. There, during an illness, he received a dramatic dream in which he was dragged into a court of the Lord and charged with being more concerned with Cicero—i.e., with pagan literature—than with Christianity. Afterward he undertook to mend his ways and became a hermit in the desert for some time, where, diverted from his desire for pagan classics, he learned Hebrew. After his return to Antioch he was ordained a priest, then went to Constantinople and later to Rome, working as a secretary to Pope Damasus. Eventually he came to Bethlehem, where he stayed until his death, running a monastery and a hostel, and studying, teaching, and providing hospitality to pilgrims.

Jerome's attitude to the cult of the martyrs can be seen in a letter he wrote attacking a priest named Vigilantius, who had apparently condemned as superstitious customs such as the veneration of relics, vigils in the churches of the martyrs, prayers offered to the dead, and the burning of tapers—criticisms similar to those that would surface more than a thousand years later, during the Reformation. In a full-blooded rebuttal, complete with Ciceronian rhetoric, Jerome responded to Vigilantius's reductive argument that it was absurd to kiss and adore the remains of saints—"a bit of powder wrapped up in a cloth"—by appealing to authority and tradition. He cited, for example, the occasion when the emperor Arcadius (c. 377–408) had taken the bones allegedly of the prophet Samuel in procession from Palestine to Constantinople and how the Christians who greeted the relics along the way were "as joyful as if they had witnessed a living prophet among them." Jerome accused Vigilantius of lacking imagination—"you are sceptical because you think only of the dead body"—and reminded him of the biblical text stating that God is not God of the dead but of the living. In denying the validity of praying to the dead, Jerome claimed, Vigilantius was denying the whole idea that those in this world were connected with the departed in a relationship of mutual help.

Jerome defended the orthodox view robustly, showing the passion and rhetoric that made him enemies and attracted his close band of friends. One of the latter was a widow named Paula, who abandoned her aristocratic life in Rome to follow him to Bethlehem. In a letter written some years after her death, Jerome gives a moving account of Paula's piety and her pilgrimages to the holy sites. She traveled from Rome by ship, stopping at places that would become familiar in later medieval pilgrim itineraries, such as the islands of Rhodes and

Cyprus. When she reached Jerusalem, she displayed a religious fervor and "concretizing" imagination that Vigilantius would have found abhorrent. "She threw herself down," Jerome says, before the True Cross "as though the Lord was hanging on it," and in Bethlehem she saw "with the eyes of faith" the baby Jesus crying in the manger and "declared she could see the slaughtered innocents, the raging Herod, Joseph and Mary fleeing into Egypt." She also visited Hebron, Bethany and the tomb of Lazarus, Jericho, the Jordan, and Samaria, where, at certain holy tombs, she witnessed demon-possessed men howling like animals and contorting their bodies, seemingly enraged by the spiritual power of the dead saints.

Paula, along with her daughter Eustochium, settled in Bethlehem, founded a convent of nuns (which Eustochium took over when her mother died in 404), and helped Jerome with his biblical scholarship. Their enthusiasm for the Holy Land is expressed in a letter they sent to a Roman widow named Marcella. In it they plead with Marcella to come and join them in Palestine, arguing that a Christian's spiritual education is incomplete if he or she has not visited Jerusalem. The letter also conjures up a picture of the spiritual power that radiated out from the Holy Land across the empire, drawing pilgrims to Jerusalem from all over the Roman world, including from Gaul and Britain.

The letter ends by trying to tempt Marcella (apparently to no avail) with all the sights she would see if she came; in doing so it gives a list of the pilgrimage places frequented at this period, including Nazareth, where Jesus grew up; Cana, where he was said to have turned water into wine; Capernaum, which he used as his base during his ministry in Galilee; the River Jordan and the Mount of Olives—scenes of Jesus's baptism and passion; and, of course, his tomb. In centuries to come, this pilgrimage trail would be augmented by the joint grave of Paula and Eustochium themselves. It lay, according to the record of a twelfth-century pilgrim named Saewulf, beneath the southern altar of the church in Bethlehem.

Jerome may have failed to tempt Marcella to travel to the Holy Land, but a century later visitors to Jerusalem were numerous enough to have inspired the creation of a pilgrim's handbook to the city, known as the *Breviarius* (c. 530), which listed some of its most sacred relics, including the Crown of Thorns, the plate on which John the Baptist's severed head had been placed, and the stones that were used to kill St. Stephen.

———

Under Constantine's successors, the church continued to expand and consolidate—the only fly in the ointment being Emperor Julian the Apostate (r. 361–363), who tried unsuccessfully to reestablish paganism as the state religion. But the church was too well entrenched for what Athanasius, bishop of Alexandria, referred to as "a little cloud and it will soon pass." It was more preoccupied with theological disputes—especially debates about the nature of Christ in relation to the Father—which were often fueled by regional politics. Paganism suffered a further blow during the reign of Emperor Theodosius I, a zealous Christian who destroyed pagan temples and outlawed sacrifices (though pagans themselves were tolerated). By the time of his death in 395, Christianity was not just the favored imperial faith: the Roman state was nothing less than a Christian state.

But while the church was busy becoming part of the imperial establishment, attracting money, property, and endowments from the wealthy, a countermovement arose in which various men and women, taking their example from the itinerant and simple lives of Jesus and the apostles, turned their backs on the world and embraced an ascetic life as monastics and hermits, often in the desert. In doing so they attracted pilgrims who sought to deepen their own spirituality.

Influential among these early solitaries was St. Antony of Egypt (c. 251–356), considered the founder of monasticism in the West, whose reputation for holiness was such that while he was still alive he became the object of pilgrimage. Born in Egypt, Antony withdrew from society as a young man to live with local ascetics and copy their way of life. In about 286 he retreated to a deserted place on a mountain near the Nile and lived there for twenty years, reputedly struggling with demons. Despite his isolation, Antony's reputation as a holy man spread far and wide, drawing pilgrims to his lonely outpost. At first he refused to see them, but many made their homes in nearby huts and caves and begged him to be their spiritual guide. Eventually, in about 305, Antony succumbed to their request and for the next several years taught and organized them into a loose-knit community obedient to a monastic rule. In the end, he again retreated into solitude, this time to a mountain near the Red Sea, where he spent the remaining years of his long life.

Another ascetic of this early period who attracted pilgrims during his lifetime was St. Simeon Stylites (c. 390–459), the famous "pillar hermit." Born in northern Syria, Simeon entered a monastery near Antioch in his teens, then left to become a solitary in a remote hut where he practiced severe austerities such as not eating or drinking and standing upright throughout Lent. From the hut, Simeon progressed to the greater solitude of the small ledge of a mountain. But the incessant numbers of pilgrims who came to seek him out compelled him to resort to even sterner measures, and he spent the rest of his life living on top of a series of pillars, the last of which was about fifty feet high.

Perhaps not surprisingly, Simeon's aim to escape the crowds backfired. Pilgrims and curious travelers flocked to see him perched on his aerie, and talismanic statuettes of the saint and medallions depicting him on his pillar became popular souvenirs. Those unable to make the journey to his pillar could communicate through letters, which were brought up to him by using a ladder. Simeon responded to his daily audience by preaching sermons or by ignoring the crowd and carrying on with his customary prayer prostrations, sometimes carrying out more than a thousand a day. He became so famous that even the Byzantine emperors Theodosius II and Leo I came to see him; he also inspired other "pillar saints" such as Daniel the Stylite (409–493), who lived on a column near Constantinople. When Simeon died, the churches of Antioch and Constantinople vied to possess his remains, with Antioch obtaining the honor. In time, a church and monastery were built around his pillar to commemorate him. Simeon showed that it was not only the "seed of the martyrs" that drew pilgrims, but also the shining example of the living ascetic.

5

CELTS AND
ANGLO-SAXONS

*"Then leaping over both threshold and mother he
[Columbanus] asked his mother not to give way to
her grief; she would never see him again in this life,
but wherever the way of salvation led him, there he
would go."*

Jonas of Bobbio, *Life* of St. Columbanus

"**M**y voice sticks in my throat; and as I dictate, sobs choke my words." So wrote St. Jerome in 410 as he remembered the recent sack of Rome by the Visigoths, one of the more notable milestones in the protracted decline and eventual fall of the Western Roman Empire. News of the capture of Rome reached Jerome in far-off Palestine, and in a letter to a woman named Principia, he described the shock of hearing that the "city which had conquered the world was itself conquered." The decline of the empire and the resulting challenges to the church had an important impact on pilgrimage, since the breakdown of central authority and law and order, as well as a crumbling infrastructure, made travel to holy places much more difficult. The two pilgrims (the Bordeaux Pilgrim and Egeria) whose travels were recorded in the fourth century were, as we have seen, from mainland Europe. After the demise of the empire it was in the lands farther west, Ireland and Britain, that pilgrims and missionaries began to stir.

Hypotheses as to why the Roman Empire in the West disintegrated are as numerous as the Germanic peoples who migrated into the empire in the fifth century CE. It has been proposed that the growth of Christianity and its pacifist ideology neutered Rome's belligerent instincts, or that the fundamental problem lay in the weakness of central government and a deterioration of the caliber of the army, or in the decline of urban life, or a downward economic spiral coupled with a punitive tax system. Unfavorable climatic conditions and epidemics of plague have also been mooted. The truth may be that all these factors played a part, and that it is too difficult to disentangle which were causes and which effects.

In any case, the immediate beneficiaries of Rome's ills were the Germanic peoples who had been living along the fringes of the empire, well aware of its relative prosperity and peace. In the late fourth century, Emperor Theodosius I had tried to negate the threat of the Goths and other Germanic peoples by permitting them to live inside the empire and giving them the status of *foederati*, or allies. But even this desperate measure failed to stem the advance of yet more Germanic peoples, themselves harried by the western movement of aggressive Central Asian tribes. Franks, Ostrogoths, Saxons, Angles, Alans, Burgundians, and others moved into almost all parts of the Western Empire as well as North Africa, where the Vandals established a kingdom.

In 476 the last Western Roman emperor, Romulus Augustulus, was deposed by the Germanic leader of the Roman Army, itself a hodgepodge of Germanic mercenaries. By the beginning of the sixth century, Germanic peoples had established kingdoms within the old empire. Certain structures of Roman culture and civilization continued, albeit in diminished forms, inspiring admiration and imitation among the new conquerors. Germanic nobles called themselves by

Roman titles and copied Roman manners and customs. They married Roman women, learned Latin, and many became (or were already) Christian. The Ostrogothic king Theodoric, who ruled Italy from 493 to 526, repaired the infrastructure of his domains and patronized the arts. In Gaul, Clovis, king of the Franks, established a strong government and around the year 500 converted to Christianity. He and his successors (known as the Merovingians after a Frankish ancestor named Merovech) laid the foundations of Frankish power, which reached a glorious climax in the rule of Emperor Charlemagne.

———

The church, with its learning and clear lines of authority, underpinned what remained of Roman civilization on continental Europe during these centuries. But the situation farther west, in Britain and Ireland, was different. Pagan Angles, Saxons, and Jutes from Scandinavia and northern Germany invaded Britain and wore down the Romano-British population, eventually establishing kingdoms in almost the entire country except the far west. In Ireland, too remote for the Germanic invaders—as it had been for the Roman legions— the Celtic people continued their pagan way of life up to the fifth century. They worshipped a number of gods, and their religious rites were ordered by a powerful priestly caste known as the Druids. Society revolved around the courts of numerous petty kings—nominally owing allegiance to a high king—who frequently fought among themselves and launched piratical raids on the west coast of Britain for slaves and other booty.

Yet in a relatively short period of time, Ireland, and a little later Britain, was to produce a stream of Christian missionaries and teachers, learned and burning with religious ardor, who sailed across to mainland Europe as evangelists, monks, hermits, scholars, and pilgrims. There they founded monasteries, churches, and hostels, spread the word of God among the pagans and semi-pagans, and strengthened the faith of their fellow Christians. How did this phenomenon come about?

Although the Irish would have come into contact with Christianity through trading connections and the capture of British slaves, it was not until 431 that Pope Celestine sent a certain Palladius to be Ireland's first bishop. How much Palladius achieved is debatable; and whatever he did do was cast in the shade by St. Patrick, also in the fifth century. A Briton by birth, Patrick was seized by Irish pirates when he was sixteen and taken off to the country he would later convert. After six years of slavery he escaped and eventually returned home; but a visionlike dream convinced him to return to Ireland as a Christian missionary. He spent the rest of his life traveling around the country, spreading the Gospel, converting local chieftains, ordaining priests, and laying solid foundations for the growth of the Irish church.

In the century following Patrick's death, great monasteries arose around Ireland, including Clonard, Clonmacnoise, Derry, Durrow, and Bangor, and Irish monks began to give up the relative security of home to set out abroad in search of new opportunities (usually in isolated and dangerous places) to fulfill their spiritual vocations. Some would set sail to remote islands—"deserts in the ocean" as they were known, such as the Orkneys off the north tip of Scotland—or set up hermitages in inhospitable regions in Britain or Europe. Some founded great monasteries, such as Luxeuil in France or St. Gall in Switzerland.

The Latin term commonly used to refer to these wandering Irish monks, *peregrinus*, meant at first simply "foreigner" but came to signify "pilgrim," though in some cases it is not clear which sense was meant. In fact some early Irish *peregrini* were convicted criminals who had been sentenced to wander abroad as exiles, sometimes forever. But the term is most usually associated with the monks and missionaries who, for several centuries, set off on their own accord into the unknown, letting God guide their footsteps or sails.

This practice of wandering without a fixed destination, for the love of God, was a variant on shrine-directed pilgrimage. Although part of the purpose of the Irish *peregrini* was to live as hermits or as missionaries, they also actively sought out the experience of traditional pilgrims: long, lonely journeys; physical hardship and danger; and the chance to visit and pray in holy places. But unlike the pilgrims on the continent, these *peregrini* were prepared, having set out, never to see their homeland again. They simply trusted God to show them the way. A good example of this attitude can be found in the *Anglo-Saxon Chronicle*, which tells how one day in 891 three Irishmen landed on the coast of Cornwall in a boat that had no oars. The men said that they wanted to "live in a state of pilgrimage, for the love of God, they cared not where." They had taken provisions for only seven days and had reached Cornwall just before their food ran out.

————

One of the great inspirational figures of these early Irish *peregrini* was St. Brendan of Clonfert (c. 486–578), known as the Navigator. Brendan's legendary voyage to the west in search of the "Island Promised to the Saints" is recounted in the tenth-century *Navigatio Sancti Brendani*, a popular Latin account that was translated into French, Breton, Flemish, Welsh, and other languages. In the story, Brendan sets sail from southwest Ireland with seventeen fellow monks, on a voyage lasting seven years. After the first forty days they arrive at the first of many islands and witness the first of many miracles: they are guided by a benevolent dog to a mysterious hall where they find jugs of water and then fish and bread laid out for them. They reach their next island on Maundy Thursday and encounter sheep the "size of bulls." Then a man suddenly appears who acts as their spiritual guide or good steward. He tells the monks they will spend the night of the coming Easter vigil on an unnamed nearby island and Easter Sunday itself on an island called the Paradise of Birds. The monks duly reach the neighboring island, but when they come to light a fire to cook their food the island starts to move (it is in fact a whale), prompting them to scramble for their boat and make off in great haste.

On the Paradise of Birds, they find a tree filled with pure white birds who can speak and sing psalms, and who turn out to be fallen angels. One of them tells Brendan that in the following years he and his men will keep returning to the same islands to celebrate Easter before eventually reaching their ultimate destination. And so it proves. The voyage continues in its inexorable circular rhythm, punctuated by surreal sights and dangerous encounters. The monks witness, for example, a fire-breathing creature destroying a sea monster, they come to an island where three choirs—of boys, youths, and men, dressed in white, blue, and purple robes, respectively—are singing psalms, and they are brought grapes the size of apples by a bird that saves them from a menacing griffin. They also sail past a huge column of pure crystal rising from the sea, they approach the grim smoking mountain of hell, and they come across a man perched on a rock out at sea—none other than Judas, who has been granted the temporary respite of the rock from the torments of hell.

Toward the end of their voyage, the monks arrive at an island where they discover the amazing 140-year-old Paul the Hermit, whose naked body is bristling all over with snow-white hair. Paul recognizes Brendan as someone specially favored by God—a propitious omen as the voyage, and the story, draws to an end. After a final Easter spent on their now-familiar islands, the monks are guided by the good steward to the Island Promised to the Saints. Negotiating a dark fog, they reach the shore and find the island full of fruit trees. They venture forth inland for forty days and finally come to a river where a young man suddenly appears, blesses them, and says that they have found their destination and now must return home. So, abruptly and without more ado, they set off back to Ireland, laden with fruit and jewels, to receive a rapturous welcome from the brethren of Clonfert.

Whether Brendan actually made a voyage approximating to that described in the *Navigatio* is still debated. During his life the saint was known for his travels around Ireland and the British Isles (and possibly Brittany). Mixed in with the *Navigatio*'s miraculous happenings are nuggets of practical information suggestive of an actual voyage: for example, Brendan's boat, we are told, consisted of a tanned oxhide stretched over a ribbed wooden frame, seams were greased with animal fat, propulsion was by sail and oars, and spare animal skins and extra fat were stored on board.

In 1976 the British explorer Tim Severin decided to test whether Brendan's voyage would have been possible with early medieval materials and technology. Building a wooden-framed, oxhide boat, he set out from Ireland to America, via the Faroe Islands, Iceland, and Greenland. Severin's epic trip, recounted in his *The Brendan*

Voyage, was a startling success. His boat, irresistibly called the *Brendan*, reached the New World, surviving saltwater attrition, stormy seas, and ice floes. Severin also suggested identifications between some of the *Navigatio's* descriptions and landmarks on his own voyage: the island of giant sheep and the Faroes, where sheep abound; the mountain of hell and the southern volcanic region of Iceland; the column of crystal and the icebergs off Greenland; and the fog-bound but ultimately fruitful Island Promised to the Saints and Newfoundland. The islands in the *Navigatio* inhabited by monks and hermits might also reflect the fact that Irish monks did actually settle in remote places such as the Hebrides, the Faroes, and Iceland. Also, the Brendan of the story resembles actual Irish *peregrini* in the way that he is prepared to entrust his vessel to God, as when he tells his men, "The Lord is our captain and helmsman, is He not? Then let Him direct us where He wills."

Severin's journey showed that it is possible the *Navigatio* drew on an actual voyage or on descriptive elements of a number of voyages. Yet the *Navigatio* is also pervaded with an atmosphere of the supernatural, a characteristic of the medieval *Lives* of saints, which mix fact with legend. In addition, the *Navigatio* draws on a rich tradition of pagan Irish stories of "adventures" (*echtrai*) and "voyages" (*immrama*), which are also filled with the miraculous. Examples include the "Voyage of Bran," in which the eponymous hero sets out to find the Land of Women, and the "Voyage of Maeldúin," in which Maeldúin, searching for his father's killer, lands on thirty-one islands where he finds, inter alia, giant ants, weeping mourners, shouting birds, and a great arc of water. There are other elements that give the *Navigatio* an air of unreality, such as the recurring symbolism of the numbers three and forty with their biblical connotations of the Trinity, the three days of Easter, and the forty days of Lent. And although Brendan resembles actual *peregrini* in some ways, he differs from them in one crucial aspect—the fact that he has a clear goal: the Island Promised to the Saints. It is this that gives the *Navigatio* its strong narrative current and sense of mission. Like Jason and the Argonauts, or Odysseus, or the heroes of the Irish *immrama*, Brendan has a specific destination in mind.

By fusing elements of an actual voyage with that of a spiritual journey the *Navigatio* straddles two worlds, one of Atlantic voyaging with echoes of the historical *peregrini*, the other of internal spiritual journeying.

———

If Brendan is the archetypal Irish spiritual sea traveler, his equivalent on land is arguably St. Columbanus (c. 543–615), who founded the important monasteries of Annegray and Luxeuil in Burgundy and Bobbio in Italy, wrote an influential monastic rule, and set an example to posterity as a fearless moralist and missionary. He referred to himself as a *peregrinus* and (according to his contemporary biographer, Jonas of Bobbio) took as his guiding light the words God spoke to Abraham in Genesis 12:1, "Leave your country, your people and your father's household and go to a land I will show you." He was essentially a free spirit, acutely aware of the fleeting nature of life on earth, and prepared to abandon security and comfort for the hardship his questing soul demanded. His whole life, with its long, hazardous physical journeys and spiritual peaks and troughs, reads like the arduous pilgrimage he believed a Christian's destiny should be.

Columbanus was born in the province of Leinster in Ireland. After a number of years at the Irish monastery of Bangor, he decided to become "an exile for the sake of Christ." In about 590 he sailed off with twelve companions (twelve being the apostolic number) to the coast of Brittany and from there made his way farther into Gaul. The band of hardy Irish missionary monks first settled in the region of Burgundy. The local king allowed them to found a monastery on a ruined Roman site known as Annegray. There they subsisted on tree bark, roots, herbs, and the charitable offerings of local people. Before long, Columbanus gained a reputation for holiness and began to attract visitors seeking cures for illnesses. When more monks swelled the ranks of the original twelve, Columbanus founded a second monastery nearby, at a place called Luxeuil. But the flow of visitors and recruits continued unabated and the saint had to establish yet another house, Fontaine, just to the north. He then divided his time between Luxeuil and Fontaine, organizing his monks along the lines of his monastic rule. Jonas also reported that Columbanus worked miracles and communicated with animals.

Eventually he encountered opposition from the local bishops, seemingly resentful of the Irishman's popularity and objecting to some of his Celtic Christian practices (notably the dating of Easter); and he also fell foul of the local king, Theodoric II. Columbanus and his Irish brethren were ordered to leave Luxeuil and return to Ireland. But when they reached Nantes near the Loire estuary, where they intended to embark for Ireland, destiny decreed otherwise. As soon as their ship set sail, a huge wave drove it back to the shore where it remained, beached like a whale, for three days. And when the captain offloaded "all that belonged to Columbanus," as Jonas wrote, a wave washed the ship out to sea and "all, filled with amazement, understood that God did not wish Columbanus to return home."

Columbanus traveled back through France and came into southwest Germany and Switzerland. At Lake Constance he preached the Gospel to the local people. He was then prompted to continue his journey after receiving a vision of an angel who showed him "in a little circle the structure of the world, just as the circle of the universe is usually drawn with a pen in a book." The angel pointed out how much of the world had yet to hear the word of God and told him that wherever he went, his missionary endeavors would be rewarded.

Around the year 612, Columbanus set off once more and reached northern Italy. (He left behind his companion Gall, who continued to preach and missionize, giving his name to the town of St. Gall in Switzerland.) Columbanus settled at a fertile spot in the Apennines known as Bobbio and founded his last monastery there. Bobbio was the end of Columbanus's long pilgrimage around Europe.

Columbanus was a giant among the early Irish *peregrini*, journeying from Ireland "for the sake of Christ." But there were many other Irishmen who went, such as the seventh-century missionaries Fiachra and Kilian. St. Fiachra established a hermitage in Breuil, east of Paris, as well as a hostel for pilgrims and travelers. (As a result of his prowess at growing vegetables, medicinal herbs, and other plants, he became the patron saint of horticulturists.) After his death in about 670, his burial place became a pilgrim destination, and in the course of time his relics were transferred to Meaux Cathedral near Paris. St. Kilian also left Ireland for continental Europe. He made his way to Germany, sailing along the Rhine and the Main to Bavaria, where he converted the local pagan ruler, Gozbert. In about 689, Kilian was supposedly murdered at the instigation of Gozbert's wife, enraged that Kilian had pronounced her marriage invalid because she was the widow of Gozbert's brother. Kilian's relics are kept in Würzburg, and the cathedral there is dedicated to him.

One of the best-recorded lives of Irish pilgrim-missionaries of this period is that of St. Fursey who, according to the near-contemporary English monk and historian Bede, vowed to "spend his life as a pilgrim for love of our Lord and to go wherever God should call him." Fursey left Ireland in about 633 and sailed to Britain to convert the pagans of England. He founded a monastery in a wooded area in the windswept flatlands of East Anglia. Then, in the 640s, he decided to migrate to Gaul with a small band of companions, where he founded a monastery in Lagny-sur-Marne near Paris. He died around 650 and was laid to rest at Péronne in Picardy where, for thirty days, pilgrims came to pay their respects to his mortal remains—which they found "incorrupt and exhaling a sweet odor." Fursey was also famous for receiving a vision of the afterlife that included a glimpse of hell, an experience that was said to have left him with physical scorch marks, as well as the propensity to sweat even in the coldest of temperatures.

If the Irish led the way as pilgrims and missionaries in various parts of western Europe, the English were not far behind them. The early medieval English were descended from British Celts and Germanic Angles (whence *Engl*and), Saxons, and Jutes, who invaded Britain after the collapse of the Roman Empire. In the course of time these pagan Anglo-Saxons were converted to Christianity, initially through the work of Irish missionaries, mainly in the north of the country. Then, in 597, a group of about forty Roman monks, under their leader Augustine (who would become the first archbishop of Canterbury), landed in Kent with orders from Pope Gregory I to evangelize the country. By 601 they had converted the local king, Ethelbert of Kent, and soon English-born, Roman-trained monks were spreading the word of God among their pagan kinsmen. In time, however, tensions arose between them and churchmen of the Celtic Christian tradition in the north (points of difference included the dating of Easter and the style of monastic tonsures). But after the synod of Whitby in 664, Rome prevailed, and orthodox English *peregrini* were heading off to the continent, like their Irish counterparts.

Two such successful itinerant English monks were Willibrord (c. 658–739) and his younger contemporary St. Boniface (c. 675–754). Willibrord was born in Northumbria and spent twelve years in Ireland before departing in 690 to evangelize Frisia (bordering the North Sea). He was supported in his mission by the Frankish ruler Pippin II and Pope Sergius I, who appointed him archbishop of Utrecht. An august, enthusiastic figure, Willibrord set about founding monasteries and churches, and challenged the local pagans by destroying their sacred cult objects. At the time of his death he had succeeded in laying the basis of Christianity in the region.

St. Boniface, possibly from Crediton in Devon, achieved even more substantial results for the faith farther east. Boniface's most famous act was cutting down a sacred pagan oak tree at Geismar (in modern Thuringia)—and because the gods seemed to let this sacrilege occur without wreaking vengeance, large numbers of pagans converted. Boniface was eventually made archbishop of Mainz and in this position he was able to name bishops, found monasteries, and generally strengthen the church in the region. He eventually died at Dokkum in Frisia in 754, where he was allegedly attacked by bandits. His remains are now kept in the cathedral of Fulda, in central Germany.

One of the vulnerable areas of the Anglo-Saxons' pagan religion had been its absence of an optimistic afterlife. Bede memorably described how one of the councillors of King Edwin of Northumbria likened a person's life to a sparrow that flies in and out of a banqueting hall, experiencing a little bit of light and warmth before returning to the darkness from which it came. Christianity, on the other hand, brought new hope with an afterlife that offered the possibility of union with God.

Yet the Christian view of what happens after death had its own sources of anxiety. The need to avoid hell and to shorten the period spent in the hell-like torments of purgatory became a major challenge for the faithful during the Middle Ages. Already by the seventh century it was a significant concern and a motive for pilgrimage. In the late 680s, Caedwalla, the king of Wessex, abdicated his throne in order to make the journey to Rome in the hope of being baptized at "the shrine of the blessed Apostles" and then ending his days shortly afterward in a blessed state. The king arrived in the Eternal City in 689, received baptism, then promptly fell ill and died, still wearing his white baptismal clothing. In a similar vein King Ine, the successor to Caedwalla on the Wessex throne, also made the pilgrimage to Rome at the end of his life, and also died there; and Bede reported that "nobles and peasants, lay people and clerics, men and women" were inspired to imitate the Roman pilgrimage of these two kings.

But the English also made pilgrimages closer to home, at local shrines. A typical sanctuary was the tomb of St. Chad in Lichfield, in central England. Not much is known about Chad, but according to Bede, he trained as a monk under Aidan, bishop of Lindisfarne, who then sent Chad to Ireland to deepen his knowledge of the faith. Later Chad became abbot of a number of monasteries and strengthened the church in the English kingdom of Mercia. After his death in 672, his remains became a focus for pilgrimage. His body lay in a tomb shaped like a small wooden house, with a hole in one side to allow pilgrims to stretch in their hands and gather dust made holy by its proximity to the saint.

Bede also recorded other instances of local pilgrimage in seventh-century England. There was, for example, a convent in Barking in Essex known as a place of healing because of the remains of various saints in its burial ground. On one occasion, according to Bede, a pilgrim regained her sight by praying at these holy relics. The remains of St. Cuthbert of Lindisfarne (d. 687) had a similar healing power. A paralyzed monk named Badudegn prayed for a cure at Cuthbert's tomb and felt the sensation of a "large, broad hand" easing the pain in his body; and a monk at a monastery in Penrith, who had a tumor on his eyelid, was healed after he applied to it a few of Cuthbert's hairs taken from his shrine.

————

In summary, during the sixth and seventh centuries Irish *peregrini*, as well as their English counterparts, crossed the English Channel as "Christ's exiles"—pilgrims, missionaries, scholars, and founders of monasteries. By the eighth century, however, the initial vigor of this movement had begun to wane and Christians on the continent were viewing Irish and English missionaries more critically. As the church became better organized and the monastic rule of St. Benedict was established throughout the Carolingian Empire, tolerance diminished for these itinerant, less predictable foreign pilgrims. As Kathleen Hughes has noted, "The traditional idea of Irish pilgrimage could no longer be accommodated in the climate of Benedictine stability."

Although Irish pilgrims still traveled to Gaul in the ninth century, they were now more likely to be making conventional pilgrimages to Rome or serving as scholars in Carolingian monasteries. At the same time, monastic reformers in Ireland, eager to exert more discipline on their brethren, were encouraging monks *not* to leave their homeland. Expressive of these new attitudes is an anonymous Irish poem of the time that declared, "There is a heavy toll / Involved in journeying to Rome / And very little gain. / The king you wish to find in Rome / You'll seek and seek in vain / Unless he travels in your soul."

6

DECLINE AND REVIVAL

"Without delay they went on steadily through the vast lands of Italy, through the depths of the valleys, the steep heights of the mountains, the level plains . . ."

Account of St. Willibald's pilgrimage
to the Holy Land

I n the seventh and eighth centuries, in the Mediterranean world, Christianity had to face the challenge of a new, expanding religion: Islam. The rise and spread of Islam was as sudden as it was momentous and had profound ramifications for Christian pilgrimage, not least because of the Muslim conquest of Palestine.

After the death of the Prophet Muhammad in 632, the Muslim faith fanned out from its heartland of Arabia. The two major powers in the Middle East at this time were the Byzantine Empire and Persia, which had worn each other out in constant warfare. Both of them were unable to resist the swift, disciplined, and zealous Muslim Arab cavalry, who inflicted defeat after defeat on them. Within decades of the Prophet's death, Muslim armies had swept eastward into Iran; north into Palestine (Jerusalem fell in 638), Syria, and eastern Turkey; and westward along the North African coast to what is now Morocco. In 711, a Muslim Arab and Berber army from North Africa crossed the Strait of Gibraltar and invaded Christian Spain, conquering most of it within a few years. By 720 they had pushed into France, but were finally halted near Poitiers in 732 by a Frankish army under Charles Martel.

Although this defeat balked the Muslim advance into northern Europe for good, Muslim rule now extended from the Atlantic Ocean to the borders of India and included many of Christianity's most holy places. How did this affect pilgrimage, in particular to the Holy Land? After the Muslims had conquered Jerusalem, Christian pilgrims at first seemed to prefer Rome as their destination. Yet over the course of time the Holy Land regained much of its popularity. One reason was that on the whole, Muslim rulers were relatively tolerant toward Jews and Christians, allowing them to practice their religion so long as they paid a poll tax. Also, because the pilgrimage to Mecca is one of the Five Pillars of Islam, Muslims could understand the motives of Christian pilgrims. A Frankish pilgrim known as Bernard the Monk, who made the pilgrimage to Jerusalem in the ninth century, said that so long as Christians had their permits in order, relations between Christians and Muslims were excellent. To illustrate this point, Bernard claimed that if a pilgrim's camel or donkey died in Palestine, he could leave his possessions where they were, go off to a town, and, on his return, find they were all safe and sound.

Equipped with documents and money for tips and bribes, it seems Western pilgrims could visit Palestine without too much difficulty. Two such pilgrims were Arculf (believed to be a bishop of Gaul) and St. Willibald, an English monk from Wessex. Arculf traveled to Jerusalem in the 680s, and during his voyage home his ship was wrecked off the coast of Scotland. He took refuge in the island monastery of Iona, where he described his Holy Land pilgrimage to the abbot Adomnan, who preserved his guest's account for posterity. Arculf had seen various holy relics and sites in Jerusalem, including what was claimed to be the lance that pierced Jesus's side and the fig tree from which Judas allegedly hanged himself. He visited the Church of the

Holy Sepulchre (he was impressed by the Anastasis) and the Church of the Ascension on the Mount of Olives.

In the early 700s, a few decades after Arculf's journey, Willibald also made a pilgrimage to Rome and the Holy Land. After a two-year stay in Rome he sailed off to Palestine by way of Sicily, the southern tip of the Greek Peloponnese, the islands of Chios and Samos, the city of Ephesus on the western coast of what is now Turkey, and the island of Cyprus. In Syria, Willibald and his party were arrested by local Muslims on suspicion of spying. Released on payment of a ransom, they traveled south via Damascus to Jerusalem. There, like Arculf, Willibald visited the Church of the Holy Sepulchre and reported seeing three wooden crosses placed outside the eastern end of the church to commemorate the crucifixion. Inside the church he was struck by the sight of fifteen oil-filled golden bowls that burned night and day inside Jesus's tomb chamber. Willibald, too, visited the Church of the Ascension on the Mount of Olives and saw there a constantly burning lantern placed at the center of the church. He also noted the local tradition that anyone who could squeeze through the narrow space between the church's columns and walls would be freed from his or her sins.

In all, Willibald spent two to three years in the Holy Land, visiting sacred sites and recovering from bouts of sickness. When he eventually left in about 726, he successfully smuggled a large pot of precious balsam past the Muslim customs officials, knowing full well that if he had been caught he probably would have been put to death. He sailed back home via Constantinople (where he stayed for two years), Sicily, and a small unnamed volcanic island to the north where he watched flames belching from the crater and plumes of smoke streaming skyward. He never returned home to England. After residing at the monastery of Monte Cassino near Naples for more than a decade, Willibald was sent by Pope Gregory III to Germany, where he became bishop of Eichstätt in Bavaria and also founded the "double" monastery (for men and women) of Heidenheim. He died in Eichstätt in 786.

———

By the time of Willibald's death, most of Western Christendom was under the sway of Charlemagne (c. 742–814), the greatest of the

Frankish kings, who, in the year 800, was crowned emperor by Pope Leo III in Rome. Charlemagne was a great champion of the Christian faith and helped to consolidate the practice of pilgrimage within his domains. During his forty-six-year rule, he expanded his territories and encouraged culture and learning. At his court in Aachen (in what is now western Germany) he gathered the leading scholars and teachers of the day, including Peter of Pisa, Paul the Deacon, and, especially, the Englishman Alcuin of York; and he made sure that monks throughout the empire were engaged in transcribing the works of the classical authors. He overhauled the administration of his empire, standardized laws, and improved the discipline of the church, imposing unity on liturgical practices.

Regarding pilgrimage, Charlemagne did much to improve conditions for missionaries and pilgrims. In 802 a decree was issued stating that pilgrims en route to their destinations must not be denied shelter or water, and in 813 it was declared at the Council of Tours that bishops must give hospitality to the poor and to pilgrims. Also, the emperor's good diplomatic relationship with the Muslim caliph Harun ar-Rashid (c. 763–809) meant he was able to build a hostel for pilgrims in Jerusalem. When Bernard the Monk visited the city in about 870, he was able to enjoy the comforts of this hostel "of the Most Glorious Emperor Charles," which was open to all pilgrims who spoke Latin. Bernard was also delighted that Charlemagne had endowed the church next door with a "magnificent library."

Bernard's chronicle is the last detailed account of a pilgrimage to Jerusalem before the period of the Crusades, which began in the late eleventh century. Setting out from Rome in the late 860s, Bernard traveled eastward across Italy to Mount Gargano, then south to Bari—at that time under Muslim rule—and Taranto, at the top of Italy's heel. From there he and his companions set sail for Alexandria. In Egypt they made their way to Farama, where the desert stretched away before them "completely white like a landscape covered in snow."

From Farama Bernard headed east, presumably by camel, to Gaza and then eventually to Jerusalem. There, on Easter Saturday, he witnessed the so-called ceremony of the Holy Fire at the Church of the Holy Sepulchre—the first recorded account of the practice, which continues to this day. As the congregation sang the *Kyrie eleison* during the morning service, supposedly an angel came and lit the lamps hanging above Jesus's sepulchre. From these flames the patriarch of Jerusalem lit the lamps of the bishops, who in turn lit the lamps of the ordinary people so that the whole church blazed with light.

Elsewhere in Jerusalem Bernard was shown a number of holy sites, including St. Simeon's Church on Mount Sion, where Jesus "washed the feet of his disciples"; the church "where we are told St. Mary died"; a church that marked the spot of St. Stephen's martyrdom, and one that commemorated Peter's threefold denial of Christ; and last but not least the church on the Mount of Olives.

After stopping off at Bethlehem and the Jordan, Bernard set sail from Joppa (Jaffa) back to Italy. In Rome he and his party visited the churches of St. John Lateran and St. Peter's (about which he said, "in terms of size no church in the world can compare to it") before continuing his journey through France. He ended it, as far as is recorded, at Mont-Saint-Michel (in Normandy). In the eighth century, St. Aubert founded an oratory there, and Bernard noted both a chapel on the islet's summit dedicated to St. Michael and the fact that no one could gain access to "the mountain until the sea recedes." Mont-Saint-Michel was to become an important pilgrim destination in later medieval times, not least because a Benedictine monastery was founded there in 966, nearly a century after Bernard's time.

While the journey to Muslim-ruled Jerusalem was relatively viable for Christian pilgrims, the holy places and pilgrimages of much of western Europe during the ninth and tenth centuries suffered from raids and invasions by Vikings. Driven by a shortage of good land at home and the lure of easy pickings abroad, pagan warriors from Denmark, Norway, and Sweden set sail in their longships—dubbed by Viking poets as "surf dragons," "oar steeds," and "fjord elks"—to plunder Britain, Ireland, France, Italy, and other parts of Europe.

The people of England were sent a warning of future Viking

depredations when, in 793, the "Northmen" or "Norsemen" burnt the monastery of Lindisfarne in the northeast of the country, slaughtered or enslaved the monks, and set off with monastic treasures. Within several years their longships were landing on the shores of Ireland. Continental Europe fared better for a little longer, probably because of the strength of Charlemagne's empire. But after the emperor's death in 814, Viking aggression increased. In 834 they raided the region of Frisia; in 836 they sacked Antwerp; five years later, Rouen was burnt; the following year it was the turn of Nantes. In 845 they attacked Paris and were paid 7,000 pounds of silver to leave and not come back—a delaying tactic also used by the English, who called their protection money "Danegeld." A contemporary Frankish monk named Ermentarius wrote that "the unstoppable flow of Vikings never stops increasing. Christians are massacred, burnt, and plundered everywhere—the undeniable evidence for which will last until the end of the world." In 860 a Viking fleet penetrated the western Mediterranean and got as far as Italy, sacking Pisa and nearby Luna. Four years later "a great heathen host," as the *Anglo-Saxon Chronicle* described it, arrived in England, ominously intent not on a swift raid but a prolonged invasion.

The Viking threat in England only came to a halt with the rise of Alfred the Great (849–899), king of Wessex, who eventually defeated the Danes and forced them to live in an area known as the Danelaw. In 911, across the sea in France, the Frankish king Charles the Simple granted lands in the northwest to Norwegian Vikings under the leadership of Rollo, hoping they would settle down and act as a bulwark against further incursions by their kinsmen. In time these Northmen gave their name to the region—Normandy—and their descendants became a formidable power in their own right.

The Vikings were not the only aggressors in Europe at this time. The Magyars, a seminomadic people from the Asian steppes, launched attacks on eastern France, southern Germany, and northern Italy, while in the Mediterranean Muslim pirates were busy ambushing Christian ships.

Eventually the turmoil of the ninth and tenth centuries eased. In

955 the German king Otto I defeated the Magyars decisively near Augsburg (Bavaria); and in the 970s a Frankish force neutralized the Muslim pirates. With the aggression of the Vikings also mostly spent, Europe could at long last breathe a sigh of relief.

The tenth century also saw a rise in the morale of the church, largely through the influence of the Burgundian monastery of Cluny. Founded in 910 in an area untouched by Viking incursions and near a major pilgrim road to Rome, Cluny prospered under its first abbots, especially St. Odo (r. 927–942), who championed monastic reforms based on a stricter interpretation of the Benedictine rule. The Cluniacs put more emphasis on the liturgy and less on manual labor and ensured that their abbots were freely elected, accountable only to the pope, and not subject to secular control. Over time the number of Cluniac daughter houses spread in France, Germany, England, Spain, and elsewhere.

Cluny was also the leading light in the "Peace of God" movement. Formulated in 989 at a council in Burgundy, it declared that anyone who attacked a member of the clergy or a church or who stole from a peasant would be excommunicated. The list of those safeguarded later also included women, children, and pilgrims. In a similar vein, further councils throughout the eleventh century continued to assert that pilgrims and other groups should not be molested but enjoy "perpetual peace." Cluny also served pilgrims in other ways, notably by establishing hospices and priories on pilgrim roads to Santiago de Compostela. By the end of the tenth century the way was being paved, almost literally, for pilgrimage to grow greatly across Europe.

7

THE NEW MILLENNIUM

"In the eighth year following the thousandth year after the Incarnation of our Savior, the relics of many saints, which had long been hidden, were revealed by various proofs and testimonies."

Ralph Glaber, *Historiae*

A s the year 1000 approached, Europeans were filled with the fear of a millennial doomsday. But shortly after the second millennium had begun, the Cluniac monk and chronicler Ralph Glaber (c. 985–c. 1047) noted that Italy, France, and other parts of Europe seemed to be celebrating the fact that the world had not come to an end by renovating and building churches, vying with each other to construct the grandest: "It was as if the entire earth had thrown off the old by shaking itself and was now clothing itself everywhere in a white cloak of churches." His words conveniently sum up the optimistic spirit of this new era. Europe had recovered from the batterings of Vikings, Magyars, and Muslims. Most of the continent was grounded in its Christian faith, apart from the Baltic region; and in Sicily and areas of Spain, the Muslims still held sway.

By the second half of the eleventh century, towns and cities were beginning to expand and craftsmen were building magnificent churches to the glory of God. The English king Edward the Confessor (c. 1003–1066) had Westminster Abbey rebuilt; in Venice, St. Mark's Basilica was refashioned in the shape of a Greek cross; in Strasbourg and Lucca, new cathedrals were erected. Santiago de Compostela was attracting more pilgrims, aided by the construction of bridges and hospices along the way. New places of pilgrimage sprang up, such as the abbey of Vézelay in Burgundy, which proclaimed that it possessed the body of Mary Magdalene, and Salerno in southern Italy, where the alleged body of the apostle St. Matthew could be visited.

The pilgrimage to the Holy Land also remained popular, even though the land continued to be under Muslim rule. The capricious caliph al-Hakim, for example, ordered the destruction of the Church of the Holy Sepulchre in 1009 and persecuted Christians. But after his death, succeeding caliphs restored the status quo and pilgrims resumed their journeys in even greater numbers—Glaber noted that the tomb of Jesus was visited by "an innumerable multitude" from all over the world, from kings down to the common people. This was partly due to the fact that the journey overland through Hungary had been much improved by the Christianization of the country by King Stephen (d. 1038). As well as monasteries and churches, Stephen built pilgrim hostels and generally improved the discipline of the clergy. Indeed, Glaber remarked that the Hungarians had turned from "cruel predators" into a people who "give freely of their own for the sake of Christ."

Nor were pilgrims to the Holy Land just individuals or small groups of travelers. In 1026 a band of some seven hundred pilgrims—sponsored by the duke of Normandy—made their way to Palestine. In late 1064, a greater number (reported to be between seven and twelve thousand souls) traveled there from Germany, led by Gunther, the bishop of Bamberg. They marched overland via Constantinople to Palestine, where, on Good Friday 1065, despite their impressive numbers, they were attacked by local bedouins near the coastal town of Caesarea. The pilgrims survived and made their way to Jerusalem. As the chronicler of the *Annals of Nieder-Altaich* wrote, "Who can explain with mere words the great flood of tears that poured forth [in Jerusalem]; who can explain how pure prayers and sacrifices they offered to God, how they sang with a joyful mind after many long-ing sighs: 'We will worship in that place, where his feet stood.'" This German pilgrim journey, with its large number of participants and conflict upon arrival, seemed to foreshadow the Crusades, the first of which began only three decades later.

————

The Crusades lasted—albeit in an increasingly attenuated form—until the end of the Middle Ages. The initial spur for them occurred when the Seljuk Turks took control of Palestine toward the end of the eleventh century and made pilgrimage there almost impossible. The Seljuks were also a threat to Byzantine security. In response, Pope Urban II (c. 1035–1099) gave a great rallying call at the Council of Clermont in November 1095. The First Crusade was set in motion, ending with the Christians' capture of Jerusalem in 1099.

Although it may seem perverse to connect a massive military oper-ation to the peaceful practice of journeying to see holy relics, the Crusades were inextricably linked with pilgrimage. The Crusaders' avowed aim was to prize Christianity's shrines from the control of the Muslims and to safeguard the journeys of pilgrims to the Holy Land; and they themselves were considered to be pilgrims, albeit of a martial kind. Like their nonmartial counterparts, Crusaders took a solemn vow to undertake their journeys, the breaking of which could result in excommunication; they also received a badge in the form of a cross from the church authorities, marking them as soldiers of Christ. In return for their service they were promised so-called indul-gences (the partial or full remission of temporal punishment due for forgiven sins), which were also the customary reward of pilgrimage. Unlike ordinary pilgrims, however, Crusaders had the possibility of plundering, thus gaining land and booty; and for many of Europe's more restless highborn young men the combination of spiritual and temporal incentives proved irresistible.

For the next two hundred years there was a permanent, although diminishing, Christian presence in the Levant. Crusader states, such as the earldoms of Edessa and Tripoli and the kingdom of Jerusalem, were established, and pilgrim traffic began to flow again. The Crusaders set about rebuilding Jerusalem, founding churches, monasteries, and convents; and in the 1140s they enlarged and amalgamated the Church of the Holy Sepulchre. It was also about this time that the two great Christian military orders of the Knights Hospitaller and Knights Templar developed, at first to give protection and hospitality to pilgrims (the Hospitallers built an enormous hospice in Jerusalem that could hold some two thousand pilgrims), then to serve as small but effective professional armies.

The Second Crusade, launched in 1147 to recapture Edessa (in what is now southeast Turkey) after its loss to the Muslims three years earlier, ended in failure. The Third Crusade (1189–92), prompted by the loss of Jerusalem, was only a partial success, with Richard I of England (the Lionheart) unable to retake Jerusalem but managing to force concessions from his adversary Saladin. The Fourth Crusade (1202–4), the last of the major expeditions, aimed to invade Egypt; but at the prompting of Venice, the army of Catholic warriors was diverted to fight against the Orthodox Christians of Byzantine Constantinople (Venice's great trading rival). In a three-day orgy of violence in April 1204 the Crusaders murdered, raped, and looted their way through the city, leaving a trail of bitterness preserved in Greek consciousness to this day.

One outcome of the Crusaders' looting of Constantinople was the redistribution of thousands of the city's precious relics to the West, where they helped to revitalize old shrines and create new ones, thus giving a boost to pilgrimage. One Latin monk is said to have stolen a wide range of relics from the Church of the Pantocrator, including a splinter of the True Cross, the arm of St. James, a tooth of St. Lawrence, a foot of St. Cosmas, and relics of more than thirty other saints. Meanwhile, the Crown of Thorns, reputedly worn by Jesus at his crucifixion, ended up in Paris, where Louis IX built the exquisite Sainte-Chapelle to house the relic.

The influence of the dispersal of Constantinople's relics is illustrated by the story of an English pilgrim named Hugh, who was returning home from the Holy Land in 1223. Passing through Constantinople, he obtained a small wooden cross, about the "size of a hand," allegedly made from a bit of the True Cross. Back in England, Hugh gave the cross to the small priory of Bromholm in Norfolk. Almost immediately the relic was said to be effecting miracles—"the blind saw, the lame walked, the lepers were cleansed"—and made Bromholm an important pilgrimage site, with visits and patronage from nobles and kings, including Henry III, Edward II, and Henry V. It even came to be mentioned in medieval literary works. In Geoffrey Chaucer's *Canterbury Tales*, one of the characters calls out in supplication, "Helpe, holy cross of Bromeholme!"; and in William Langland's fourteenth-century allegorical poem *The Vision of Piers Plowman*, there is a line about going to Bromholm "to bid the Roode [cross] of Bromholm bring me out of debt." The relic continued to draw pilgrims to the priory until its closure during the Reformation in the sixteenth century.

8

PILGRIMAGE, RELICS, AND THE AFTERLIFE

"We see small relics and a little blood. But truth perceives that these tiny things are brighter than the sun."

Victricius, bishop of Rouen in the fourth century

M edieval pilgrims, much like pilgrims today, had a variety of motives for going on their sacred journey. But central to the medieval world were questions of sin and life after death, and how people might escape from, or reduce their time in, purgatory—the dreaded state or place in the afterlife in which the soul was painfully purified before it could proceed to heaven. Thus the medieval pilgrimage "economy" involved the interrelationship between the cult of saints and their relics, purgatory, and the purging of sins.

Medieval men and women believed that after death they went to one of three "places": heaven if they were truly righteous, hell if they were unrepentant sinners, and purgatory if they fell between the saintly and the damned—which meant nearly everyone. The church explicitly publicized the rewards of saints and the torments of sinners through sermons; in church frescoes, stained-glass windows, and stone sculptures; in written accounts and manuscript illuminations. Some writings about the afterlife were literary creations, such as Dante's *Divine Comedy*, while others were penned or inspired by individuals who claimed to have had visions of the world to come. In one typical example, Bede tells the story of a Northumbrian man named Drycthelm who became a monk at Melrose in Scotland after receiving a vision of the afterlife.

Drycthelm claimed that an angelic guide had led him off to a valley in which people's souls were tossed from the fires on one side to the snow and hail on the other. He was then taken to a dark place where, amid a terrible stench and the sound of demonic laughter and cries of agony, black flames bearing the souls of men "like sparks" streamed up and down from a pit. To his relief, Drycthelm was then escorted to a fragrant meadow where people dressed in white robes were sitting happily. From there they passed to the threshold of another place where the sweet singing and the lovely scent and light were too wonderful to describe. The guide then explained to Drycthelm that the valley of heat and cold was the place where souls who were penitent only at the hour of their death had to stay before being admitted to heaven; that the pit with its black flames was the mouth of hell; the meadow was for souls who had been good when alive but did not deserve immediate entry into heaven; and the place of light was heaven itself.

Although purgatory—Drycthelm's fiery and freezing valley—did not claim the dead for eternity, as hell was thought to do, it was still a terrifying prospect. St. Thomas Aquinas remarked that no pain on earth came near the torment of its fire. But how and when did the idea of purgatory arise? There is some evidence for such a place in classical literature and the Hebrew Bible. In Virgil's *Aeneid*, Aeneas enters the underworld where the ghost of his father, Anchises, tells him about the mysteries of the dead and how souls are punished for old sins—some have their wickedness washed away, others have it burnt out of them—before being allowed to enter Elysium. In the Hebrew Bible, purgatory is suggested in the Second Book of Maccabees 12:39–45, when Judas Maccabeus and his troops pray for their dead comrades so that their sin (of wearing magic amulets) might be "entirely blotted out." Judas also sends a collection of money to Jerusalem to be offered for their sin—an action, as Christian commentators argued, that presupposes that the dead could benefit from it.

Christians also found justifications for purgatory in church tradition and in the New Testament, such as Jesus's warning in Matthew 12:32 that he who speaks against the Holy Spirit will not be forgiven in this world—or in the world to come. And St. Paul in his First Letter to the Corinthians 3:11–15 seems to imply a postmortem state where souls will be purified by fire. There was also the age-old Christian custom of praying for the dead, evident, for example, in inscriptions on tombs in the Roman catacombs: why pray for the departed, it was argued, unless they were in a place where they could be helped by prayer? St. Augustine of Hippo (354–430) summed it up by stating that prayer could help the dead who had not been so wicked while alive that they forfeited compassion, nor so good that they did not need it at all. This was the same view as that of Drycthelm's angelic guide, who said that "many are helped by the prayers, alms, and fasting of the living, and especially by the offerings of masses, and are therefore set free before the Day of Judgment."

Behind these beliefs was the idea of penance (the word comes from *poena*, Latin for "punishment"). Although the church had the power to absolve repentant sinners who confessed their wrongdoings of guilt, the miscreants were still obliged to do a penance, such as undertake a fast or a pilgrimage. For example, during the reign of the English king Canute (r. 1016–1035), it was decreed that if a priest committed a murder or any other serious crime he would have to make "as long a pilgrimage as the pope commands." In 1283 Archbishop Pecham of Canterbury decreed that a local church rector named Roger, who was found guilty of fornication, would have to spend three years going on pilgrimages to Santiago de Compostela, Rome, and Cologne as a penance.

But what happened if people died before doing their penitential punishment? The church's answer was that they would suffer their

penalty in purgatory, where they would be purged, or spiritually purified, before being admitted to the ranks of the blessed. The dead could
shorten their time in purgatory, however, if the living prayed or said
masses for them. The English mystic and pilgrim Margery Kempe (c.
1373–c. 1440) remarked that the soul of her husband would remain
in purgatory for thirty years "unless he had better friends on earth."
St. Bridget of Sweden, after her pilgrimage to Jerusalem in the early
1370s, was mystically informed that many souls in purgatory had
been freed by her pious acts in the Church of the Holy Sepulchre.
And many a will was drawn up to ensure that money would be available for pilgrimages or other acts of piety to be performed on behalf of
the deceased. Those who could afford it also often founded "chantry"
chapels so that masses could be held for their souls.

The concept of indulgences was connected with the system of penance. Over time the church recognized that some penances, particularly the longer ones, could be disruptive to the tasks of everyday life
such as plowing or harvesting, and allowed them to be commuted. So
the short, sharp shock of a flogging could be taken instead of a long
pilgrimage; or singing psalms while bending the knees could take the
place of a monthlong fast on bread and water. In civil courts it was
not uncommon for the convicted to pay a fine instead of the pilgrimage to which they had been sentenced. Books known as Penitentials
set out precisely the values of penances. The *Penitential* of Egbert, an
eighth-century archbishop of York, for example, stated that reciting
fifty psalms while kneeling down was the equivalent of fasting on
bread and water for a day, and that a yearlong fast could be reduced
by the payment of twenty-five shillings.

From about the late eleventh century onward, indulgences of specific value were assigned to certain pious acts, relics, shrines, and pilgrimages. It was said that two pilgrimages to St. David's Cathedral
in Wales were worth the virtue of one to Rome. In the late fourteenth century, traveling to Rome to pray before the relic known as
the Veronica (the legendary veil bearing the image of the face of Jesus)
was worth twelve thousand years' remission of purgatorial punish-

ment in the afterlife (but only three thousand if you were a Roman citizen). Notice boards outside churches and shrines advertised their indulgences, and handbooks called *libri indulgentiarum* were produced to list the indulgences attached to each shrine or relic. When the churchman Gerald of Wales made a pilgrimage to Rome in about 1204, he was able to calculate that during his stay he had earned indulgences worth ninety-two years. Naturally, proprietors of shrines vied with each other to pay their bishops or the pope for the privilege of dispensing indulgences, hoping to recoup their investment by the offerings donated by increased numbers of pilgrims.

The church also had at its disposal plenary indulgences, which offered a *complete* remission of penance. The first pope to do so was Urban II, who, in 1095, dispensed a plenary indulgence to those who agreed to join the First Crusade. In 1300 Pope Boniface VIII established the Jubilee Year (a special church year of remission of sins and universal pardon) and granted a plenary indulgence to all pilgrims who came to Rome, a practice that was repeated in subsequent Jubilee Years.

Over the course of time it became increasingly common for individuals to be able to buy indulgences without having to go to a shrine or see a relic. For those who were too sick or old—or too preoccupied—to go on a pilgrimage or crusade, or who could not find a substitute person to go for them, purchasing indulgences was a boon. Nevertheless, although much of the money the church raised from indulgences often went to good causes, such as the building of a hospice or bridge, the practice was open to abuse. For the rich and idle it was far easier to buy a postmortem remission of punishment rather than earn it by physical hardship; and there were those who were only too keen to make money from selling indulgences, including impecunious popes such as Boniface IX (r. 1389–1404). Official indulgence sellers known as pardoners became a familiar sight in towns and villages, where they used eloquence, impressive-looking documents, and collections of relics to persuade people to reduce their stint of purgatorial punishment—at a fee. The church recognized these faults: the Fourth Lateran Council, in 1215, for example, declared that bishops could only give indulgences worth a maximum of one year and only to those who had attended the consecration of a church; and the Council of Constance (1414–18) also tried to restrict them. Nevertheless, the abuses continued up to the Reformation.

————

The importance of relics in medieval life is shown by a story about the twelfth-century bishop Hugh of Lincoln. We are told that while visiting the monastery of Fécamp in Normandy, Hugh asked to see the monks' prize relic—the alleged arm of Mary Magdalene. On being shown the arm, Hugh promptly cut away its covering and tried to break off a piece of the bone, but in vain. Undeterred, he tried another approach and managed to bite off one of the fingers of the precious relic—much to the horror of the monks, who compared him to a dog with a bone. It should be pointed out that Hugh (who succeeded in mollifying his hosts) was not a brutish lout but a man famous for his piety, love for humanity, and kindness to lepers. He was even canonized twenty years after his death.

Relics were the tangible remains of a saint whose intercessions with God offered the hope of miraculous cures and good fortune. In an age when people took for granted the power of the supernatural and believed that common and uncommon occurrences, from sprained ankles to lightning bolts and plagues, were governed by God, relics were widely regarded as physical manifestations of the spiritual. They were objects of awe, and were often used instead of the Bible for the taking of oaths. Relics were the heart of a shrine and its crown jewels, having the power to lure pilgrims on long journeys across seas and over mountains and, when they arrived, to persuade them to part with their money. The acquisition of a relic could raise a shrine from obscurity to fame and prosperity, as happened to the priory of Bromholm.

The desire for relics was constant, and competition to obtain them could be intense—to the point of illegality. It was not uncommon for the guardians of one shrine to steal additional relics from another, and stories of wonder-working relics were used as propaganda by rival sanctuaries. In the ninth century, for instance, the monks of the abbey of Conques in southwest France coveted the relics of St. Foy (a fourth-century female martyr) owned by the monks of Agen (about a hundred miles to the west). So Conques sent an "undercover" monk to join the Agen community, and after gaining the community's trust over a number of years, this man eventually stole the relics and took them back to Conques—thereby turning it into a major pilgrimage center on the route to Santiago de Compostela.

The use of relics occurred in the first centuries of Christianity and, by the early Middle Ages, they had become essential items in worship. Bede tells how Pope Gregory I sent to Augustine of Canterbury everything he would need for church services in England, including vestments, books, vessels, ornaments, altar cloths, and "relics of the holy Apostles and martyrs." In 787, the Second Council of Nicaea increased the need for relics by decreeing that every newly built church would need a relic before it could be consecrated. This growing demand was fed during the time of the Crusades by the many relics Crusaders brought back from the Holy Land and other places.

Over time some relics gained more fame and prestige than others, attracting pilgrims from far and wide. These included what were alleged to be the tunic of the Virgin Mary at Chartres, the remains of the three Magi at Cologne, and the remains of St. James at Santiago de Compostela. Tens of thousands of other alleged relics were scattered throughout Europe's churches and shrines, including nails and splinters from the True Cross; bones, teeth, and hair and nail clippings of countless saints; vials containing the blood or even the breath of Jesus, or the milk of the Virgin Mary; bits of cloth from Mary's tunic; and so on. There were said to be some seven hundred known spikes from the Crown of Thorns. The one kept at Angers in France was actually an ordinary thorn that had merely touched the "real" Crown, which suggests a belief in the transference of spiritual power that may account for other multiplications of relics, such as the holy nails of the True Cross, of which there were at least thirty in existence.

Relics were usually kept in resplendent reliquaries, ranging from large gold-plated chests encrusted with jewels, such as at St. Thomas Becket's shrine at Canterbury, to gilt arm-shaped cases enclosing the arm bones of saints, or small pendants containing strands of holy hair. Reliquaries inspired awe and were displayed or carried in procession on special occasions such as feast days or at times of plague or national crisis. In an age of widespread illiteracy, visual impact played an important part in religion: what medieval pilgrims expected to see at the end of their journeys was something opulent and lustrous that would convey in physical terms the essence of the shrine's and the saint's spirituality. They were not so concerned with the authenticity of a relic (or whether it had been stolen from another shrine); what mattered was their own personal relationship with the sacred object, and how it connected them to the departed saint and through him or her to Christ in heaven.

The nature of this relationship, and whether reverence for someone's bones might verge on the sin of idolatry, was debated by theologians. St. Thomas Aquinas, following St. Jerome and St. Augustine of Hippo, wrote that it was normal to honor objects connected with people who had themselves been held in honor, and so it was natural to venerate the bodies of saints: "God fittingly does honor to such relics by performing miracles in their presence." Relics, therefore, were not simply objects of magic that worked their power indifferently, but receptacles of the holy presence "through which," as the Council of Trent (1545–63) later pronounced, "many benefits are bestowed on mankind."

Inevitably, however, the incessant demand for relics by churches and other religious institutions (and by wealthy individuals who wished to reap spiritual benefit from them) fueled a trade in which the distinctions between "false" and "true" relics became blurred. The church acknowledged the problem: already St. Augustine had denounced itinerants who were dressing up as monks and selling false relics for a living. But it was not always easy for church authorities to distinguish between the false and the genuine. One test of authenticity was to see whether the relic burned, since true relics were believed to resist fire: a tenth-century bishop of Trier tested the alleged body of St. Celsus during mass by casting part of the saint's finger into a censer of burning coals, which apparently did it no harm.

In the thirteenth century, the church went further to address the issue of relics. The Fourth Lateran Council decreed that ancient relics must not be displayed outside their reliquaries or put up for sale, and that newly discovered relics had to be approved by the pope. In the next century, Chaucer satirized the trade in false relics through his portrait of a pardoner in his *Canterbury Tales*. Chaucer's character has a relic collection that includes a pillow case he claims to be the veil of the Virgin Mary and various "pigs' bones" that he is passing off as the remains of saints. Boccaccio, in his *Decameron*, presents a pardoner who has a parrot's feather he pretends has come from the wings of the angel Gabriel, and a vial containing the sound of the bells of King Solomon's Temple. Although these literary examples were intended to amuse, they suggest that spurious relics were commonplace. Just how commonplace may be inferred from the inventory of relics made in 1523 at the church of Wittenberg in Germany, the epicenter of the Reformation: it showed that here, Frederick III, Elector of Saxony, had accumulated some seventeen thousand objects of veneration.

By the time of Frederick III, there were those who were openly mocking relics, including Desiderius Erasmus (c. 1466–1536), the Dutch Renaissance scholar and satirist, who was otherwise a devout Catholic. The Protestant reformers had no time for relics, nor for purgatory and the cult of the saints. For them the word of God was paramount and any practice not supported by the scriptures was at the very least suspect. This attitude, in the 1500s, would have a radical effect on relics and pilgrimage. As Erasmus wrote, "You make much of a piece of his [St. Paul's] body visible through a glass covering, and you do not marvel at the whole mind of Paul shining through his writings?"

9

ON THE ROAD

"When in April the sweet showers fall [. . .]
Then people long to go on pilgrimages . . ."

Geoffrey Chaucer, *The Canterbury Tales*

Before embarking on a long-distance pilgrimage, a medieval pilgrim had to make a number of preparations. Medieval society was highly hierarchical, with the king and his nobles at the top and peasants at the bottom, and involved a web of feudal relationships based on services owed or owing. Thus would-be pilgrims first of all had to obtain permission to leave home from their lord, or from the local bishop, abbot, parish priest, or other authority. The German friar Felix Fabri, for example, had to obtain permission from Pope Sixtus IV as well as from senior members of his Dominican order before setting off to the Holy Land in the 1480s; and when Margery Kempe was on pilgrimage in York, she was interrogated by church officials as to whether she had written permission from her husband to be there.

In England in 1388, Richard II's government decreed on pain of arrest that pilgrims should have special permits as well as passports if they wished to travel abroad. Port officials who turned a blind eye to

unlicensed pilgrims were liable to severe punishment. Official autho-
rization to travel not only helped the governing classes keep an eye on
their subjects; in an age when roads might be frequented by beggars,
runaways, and outlaws, it was also to pilgrims' great advantage to have
documents that showed the spiritual purpose of their journey. Furthermore, in most countries, at least in principle, pilgrims received special
protection as well as other legal privileges, such as exemption from certain tolls along the way.

Since pilgrimages to faraway shrines would probably involve dangers
of one sort or another, prudent pilgrims would settle their affairs before
leaving home. Debts were paid, a will was drawn up, and provision was
made for dependents. Margery Kempe, for example, asked her parish
priest to announce in church that she was going on pilgrimage and that
her creditors should come and see her before her departure.

A pilgrim's traditional clothes and accessories also had to be obtained.
These comprised a wide-brimmed hat, which gave good protection
from sun and rain; a scrip, which was a leather satchel in which documents, money, food, and knickknacks were kept; a stout staff, which
served as an alpenstock when climbing mountains, as a support in
crossing streams, and as a weapon against brigands or fierce dogs; and a
long, thick cloak that could double as a blanket. Strong boots or shoes
were indispensable, as was a water bottle or leather beaker.

These pilgrim items were more than practical aids. Before a pilgrim's departure, the staff and scrip were blessed by a priest as part
of a church ceremony, so that they would give spiritual protection.
According to the *Sarum Missal* (a liturgical book), the pilgrim first
confessed his or her sins, then lay on the floor before the altar as
the priest and choir sang suitable psalms, such as Psalm 24, which
includes the lines, "Who shall ascend into the hill of the Lord? Who
shall stand in his holy place? He that hath clean hands, and a pure
heart; who hath not lifted up his soul unto vanity, nor sworn deceit-
fully." The priest then blessed the scrip and the staff, invoking the
protection of Christ. He sprinkled holy water on the scrip and, saying
more prayers, placed it around the pilgrim's neck. He anointed the
staff and handed it over with the words, "Take this staff as a support

during your journey and the toils of your pilgrimage, that you may be victorious against the bands of the enemy and safely arrive at the shrine of the saints to which you wish to go and, your journey accomplished, may return to us in good health."

Pilgrims bound for Jerusalem would usually have cloth crosses blessed and anointed with holy water and then sewn onto their hats and cloaks before the congregation. Some of the pilgrim items also acquired symbolic value, a tendency perhaps best known from Sir Walter Raleigh's poem "The Passionate Man's Pilgrimage": "Give me my scallop-shell of quiet, / My staff of faith to walk upon, / My scrip of joy, immortal diet, / My bottle of salvation, / My gown of glory, hope's true gage; / And thus I'll take my pilgrimage."

Because pilgrims could be away for months—a typical journey from London to Rome could take several months, depending on conditions—they had to ensure they had enough money for food and lodging, for making offerings at shrines, and for buying souvenirs. For the poor this meant saving up for years on end, unless they were lucky enough to find a wealthy patron. Some pilgrims who had land might make over part or all of their property to a monastery or other landowner in exchange for cash. Another source of funding might be a trade or religious guild. In the cathedral city of Lincoln, those who belonged to the religious Guild of the Resurrection were obliged to give a halfpenny to any fellow member wanting to make a pilgrimage to Rome, Santiago de Compostela, or Jerusalem; and members of the tailors' guild each gave a penny to those bound for the Holy Land. These offerings were not entirely altruistic: by the act of giving, those unable to make the pilgrimage could identify themselves with it and share the virtue accrued by the pilgrim in the fulfillment of the journey.

The actual send-off could be small and low-key or involve a cheering crowd of family, friends, and fellow guild members, all walking with the pilgrim to the city gate or edge of town. Since it was accepted that a pilgrim might not survive a long-distance journey, emotional farewells must have been common. When Felix Fabri, during a sermon he gave in Ulm in April 1480, announced his intention to go to the Holy Land, the congregation's singing was punctuated by loud sobs as people realized the implications of his plan. Fabri set off for Venice (from where he would proceed by galley to Jerusalem), but not before he had "rushed into the arms" of his "most kind and beloved spiritual father." The two men embraced each other, their cheeks wet with tears. Then, as he departed, Fabri felt what many other pilgrims must have felt before and after him—a deep sense of futility and a sudden nostalgia for home and familiar things. The ardor with which he had yearned to see the Holy Land not only cooled but "died" within him, and the pilgrimage seemed "useless" and "empty," the memory of Ulm so much sweeter than the prospect of Jerusalem. But these feelings seem not to have stayed with him—in 1483–84 Fabri in fact went on a second pilgrimage to the Holy Land.

———

Medieval pilgrims who traveled by land would proceed on foot, or by horse, donkey, or mule, or in a wagon. They would cover approximately fifteen to twenty-five miles a day if they were walking; or from twenty to thirty miles riding at a "canter" (a word supposedly derived from "Canterbury trot," to describe the gentle pace at which pilgrims rode to Becket's shrine). Each day pilgrims aimed to arrive at an inn, monastery, or hospice before night fell; otherwise the sheer intensity of darkness—almost unimaginable now in most parts of the developed world—coupled with a lack of road signs and maps, and possible robberies, might prove their undoing. There was also danger from wolves and other wild animals. It is said that when Sturmi, an eighth-century abbot of Fulda in Germany, was traveling through the wild terrain that lay around his monastery, he had to chop down trees at the end of each day and make a stockade to protect his horse.

In medieval Europe roads were often no more than rubble tracks. Gone were the days of ancient Rome when paved roads crisscrossed the empire in straight military lines. There was no consistent central policy for maintaining roads. In fourteenth-century England they were the responsibility of local landlords, and their condition was subject to a lord's wealth and whim. Yet the construction of roads and bridges came to be viewed as a holy and virtuous duty, an act of charity comparable to giving money to the poor. It was at least partly in this spirit that the abbey of Cluny financed improvements and repairs to the pilgrim road to Santiago de Compostela. Nevertheless, the king sometimes had to intervene if the local authorities failed to fulfill their responsibilities. Charles VI of France (1368–1422) was forced to act when the roads around Paris had deteriorated into an obstacle course of boulders and deep ruts, with trees growing in the middle of the road and hedges and brambles encroaching from the sides. The king ordered the provost of Paris to carry out the necessary clearances and repairs, authorizing him to press-gang local labor if required.

Apart from the state of the roads, pilgrims and other travelers had to contend with robbers and brigands, who knew the pilgrim routes well and could easily pick off a lone pilgrim, then melt back quickly into the surrounding woods or undergrowth. In southern England the Pilgrim's Way, from Winchester to Canterbury, passed by the notorious Alice Holt Woods where robbers preyed on travelers. On the days that St. Giles' Fair was held in Winchester, mounted guards were sent by the fair's authorities to protect incoming merchants. Another measure to foil ambushes and muggings was taken in 1285 by Edward I, who ordered roadsides to be cleared by no less than two hundred feet to deprive malefactors of potential hiding places.

Pilgrims also had to contend with ongoing wars or civil strife. In the Holy Land, even after the Crusaders' conquests, bedouin tribesmen were known to swoop down on unsuspecting pilgrim bands. Some pilgrims of high rank prudently adopted humbler dress, the better to travel unnoticed. Certainly, a change of identity seems to have saved the skin of an English monk named Samson in 1161. He was traveling in Italy on his way to Rome when he found himself caught up in fighting between Pope Alexander III and Emperor Frederick I. The emperor's men were mutilating those they found traveling to the pope. Samson managed to ward off attackers by pretending to be a Scot, brandishing his stick at them "in the manner of a weapon called a gaveloc" and growling threats "in the Scottish manner."

If roads could sometimes be as much a hindrance as a medium of progress, another potential impediment to pilgrims was rivers—since bridges were not a frequent sight in the Middle Ages. If the river lacked a bridge, but was not too deep, travelers could wade across, perhaps aided by a rope strung from bank to bank. If the river was too deep or the current too strong, the only way of crossing it was by ferry, which could also be a life-endangering experience. The twelfth-century *Pilgrim's Guide* (to Santiago de Compostela) tells of the boatmen of two rivers in southwest France who extracted high charges for their services (if necessary by force) and whose boats were so small—carved from single tree trunks—that passengers were terrified the vessels would capsize. (The *Pilgrim's Guide* goes so far as to accuse the boatmen of deliberate overcrowding in order to drown passengers and steal their belongings.)

Even if ferrymen were not actively malign, they might be prone to misjudgment or callous greed. In the twelfth century, a number of fatal accidents connected to the ferry service across the River Arno in Italy prompted the saintly Allucius of Pescia to petition the local bishop to build a bridge. And a German woman crossing the Rhône on her way back from Santiago found herself on a large boat packed with about four hundred people and their horses and donkeys. As soon as the vessel hit a patch of choppy water the weight proved too much—it shipped water and sank. The woman was the only survivor.

Conditions of travel could be just as precarious in the mountains, especially the Alps, where a constant flow of pilgrims negotiated the vertiginous icy passes on their way to or from Rome. Experienced local guides, properly equipped with studded boots, were indispensable. Nonetheless, travelers often had to swap dignity for necessity and scrabble on all fours over the slippery frozen tracks. Homemade sledges made out of oxhides or branches tied together were used. Wagons had to be let down gently by rope, counterbalanced by teams of men or oxen. Avalanches were a constant hazard: in 1128 two Belgian abbots witnessed a mass of snow crashing down on the alpine village of Saint-Rémy in which houses were swallowed up and inhabitants and travelers buried alive.

Travel overland had its discomforts and dangers—but passage by ship was often worse. Pilgrim vessels regularly departed from Venice to Palestine and from English ports such as Bristol, Dartmouth, and Southampton to northern Spain, en route to Santiago de Compostela. Life on board ship for landlubbers was usually disconcerting and often distressing. For first-time voyagers the whining creak of timbers, the sudden crashing of waves, and the stench from the bilges were a novel form of endurance. Food was often maggot-ridden, and drinking water discolored and malodorous. A fifteenth-century English poem called "The Pilgrims' Sea Voyage and Seasickness" describes how gruesome the journey to Spain could be: the seasick pilgrims groan and vomit or shout for Malmsey wine to settle their stomachs; some peck at a little salted toast, others try in vain to read. The poem ends with the pilgrim narrator thinking fondly of dry land and cursing the smell from the bilge pump: "I had as lefe be in the wood / Without mete and drynk; / For when that we shall go to bedde, / The pumpe was nygh oure beddes hede, / A man were as good to be dede / As smell thereof the stynk!"

Sea journeys to Palestine were no better, as Felix Fabri recounted. As well as the heat, smell, cramped conditions, and sudden Mediterranean storms, there was also the routine threat of Muslim pirates. A German chronicle records that in 1453 a ship returning from Palestine with about three hundred pilgrims was set upon by Muslims, who killed the men and enslaved the women.

But journeys by sea could be improved a good deal—if you knew how. The seasoned fifteenth-century English pilgrim William Wey recorded some sensible tips. He recommended that pilgrims to Jerusalem should negotiate with the ship's captain for a place on the top deck, the lowest one being "ryght smolderyng hote and stynkynge." Before the start of the voyage the pilgrim should buy certain items such as sheets, pillows, a mattress, and a quilt. A good chest with a lock was essential, and a little cauldron, frying pan, plates, wooden saucers, cups, and a bread grater would not come amiss. It was sensible to take a cage with half a dozen hens, as well as a range of medical remedies such as "laxatives" and "restoratives," and various spices such as ginger, pepper, saffron, and cloves to make the food more palatable and to ease digestion. With purchases such as these, wealthier pilgrims could make conditions on board more tolerable.

As a day of traveling drew to an end, pilgrims would hope to find themselves near appropriate accommodation, be that a monastery guesthouse, hospice, or inn. Monasteries were obliged, in theory, to give free board and lodging for up to three days to pilgrims and other wayfarers. According to the Rule of St. Benedict, guests at monasteries were to be received as if they were Christ himself, and their feet washed by the abbot and his brethren. However, the hierarchical nature of medieval society meant that guests received the degree of hospitality appropriate to their rank, as shown by the monastery of St. Gall in Switzerland, which had separate accommodation for the poor, visiting monks, and high officials, who were assigned their own well-heated house with a kitchen, wine cellar, and bakery.

Along well-trodden pilgrim routes and other major thoroughfares, basic accommodation for pilgrims was provided by hostels known as *hospitia*, or hospices, many of them founded by philanthropic nobles or the Knights Hospitaller. The three most famous hospices, according to the *Pilgrim's Guide*, were in Jerusalem, at the Great St. Bernard Pass in the Alps, and at the Somport Pass in the Pyrenees (on the way to Santiago de Compostela). Several nations, including the Spanish, Swedish, and English, established their own hospices in Rome for the use of poor pilgrims from their respective countries. The English, in fact, had two hospices, one dedicated to St. Thomas of Canterbury, the other to St. Edmund, which by 1449 had grown to incorporate nine houses along with gardens and vineyards.

For pilgrims who had a bit of money, inns and taverns could prove a more congenial alternative to hospices. Inns ranged from small, dingy hovels to relatively grand establishments that might offer not only board, lodging, and stabling but also medicines and a laundry service. It was common practice for guests to share not only rooms but also beds. Each bed usually slept a minimum of two, though three to five people sharing a bed was not uncommon. (A fourteenth-century French traveler remarked that German inns customarily assigned three to a bed, while in the English town of Ware an inn named The Saracen's Head had the so-called Great Bed, which measured eleven feet long by ten feet wide and was said to hold twenty people.) Bedding could range from straw-stuffed mattresses to a heap of dried bracken; fleas, bedbugs, mice, even rats were commonly included.

A typical inn consisted of a communal area with tables and a fireplace, a kitchen, the private quarters of the innkeeper and his family, and one or more rooms for guests. Food at humble establishments included staples such as soup, bread, cheese, eggs, and poultry, while large inns in cities might provide more variety and spices to enliven the dishes. They might also supply in-house entertainment in the form of local musicians or buskers, who passed a hat around after the performance. Felix Fabri described an evening in an inn (in Trent in northern Italy), en route to Venice and the Holy Land in 1483, when he and his entourage were entertained by a local craftsman and his wife who sang, played the flute, and clowned around, much to the hilarity of the diners. In England, inns were supplemented by the alehouse or "alestake," recognizable by the long pole projecting from above the door, its tip garlanded with brushwood. Frequently found at crossroads as well as by the wayside, ale-stakes tended to be little more than humble shacks. Some offered ale alone, while others also provided basic victuals, as Chaucer's pardoner bears witness: "But first, he said, here at this ale-stake / I will both drink and bite upon a cake."

In large cities, some inns were run by expatriates who especially welcomed the company of their fellow countrymen. In Venice, the gathering place for Germans was the St. George, where even the servants were German or at least German-speaking. When Felix Fabri visited it he noted that the innkeeper's big black dog welcomed German visitors by jumping up and wagging his tail. Only Germans, however, and respectable ones at that, were shown such warmth. Beggars and other nationalities—including the native Italians—were met by growls and barking.

Innkeepers themselves were frequently the objects of complaint—not many of them were like genial Harry Bailey, the host of the Tabard Inn in *The Canterbury Tales*. Many gained a dubious reputation for charging too much for their services, especially when occasions such as Jubilee Years increased the number of pilgrims. In 1235 the

Senate in Rome passed measures in order to halt the innkeepers' practice of physically forcing pilgrims inside their inns or snatching them from rival taverns; and in England during the reign of Edward III (r. 1327–1377) a statute was passed to prevent innkeepers from selling their food at extortionate prices.

Of course, being able to speak a few words of the local language was invaluable for negotiating with hostellers, if not their dogs. Although educated pilgrims would normally speak Latin to their peers, they and their uneducated brethren would have to learn a little of the vernacular if they wanted to communicate with the locals.

A time-honored alternative to speech was sign language; another was to resort to a phrase book, a genre that became increasingly popular toward the end of the Middle Ages. The early medieval phrase book *Conversations in Old High-German*, for instance, was intended for travelers from Romance countries visiting Germany and included useful phrases such as "I would like drink," "Have you any fodder for my horse?" and "My shoe needs mending." There were also phrases such as "The Latin people are stupid, but the Bavarians are wise," which show, as Norbert Ohler has noted, "that the Romance-speaking author knew how to gain the sympathy of the 'natives.'" William Wey obligingly recorded Greek phrases that could be used on the voyage to Jerusalem in places like the islands of Crete, Rhodes, and Cyprus. Wey also noted some Arabic phrases, as did the anonymous author of the fifteenth-century English *Informacyon for Pylgrymes*. By this period there were also French-Arabic phrase books for francophone travelers.

————

When pilgrims finally reached the end of their journey and arrived at the shrine that had for days, weeks, or months been the focus of their hopes, it was clearly a moment of intense emotion. Felix Fabri, for instance, chronicles the wailing, sobbing, and convulsive fits of his fellow pilgrims at the threshold of the Church of the Holy Sepulchre in Jerusalem. For many pilgrims, cathedrals and other major churches would have been the largest and most magnificent buildings they had ever seen. The profusion of soaring columns, paintings and carvings of biblical scenes, stained-glass windows, chapels, altars, and golden bejeweled shrines bathed in the flickering light of candles must have been an unprecedented sensory experience.

During the pilgrim season and especially on saints' feast days, shrines could be crowded, noisy, and chaotic. An anonymous fourteenth-century English visitor to St. Peter's in Rome said that a pilgrim might have to search all day for a lost companion, so vast was the church and so great the number of visitors running hither and thither, collecting indulgences at various shrines and altars.

The sick would press their way toward a shrine on crutches, the paralyzed with the help of hand-trestles, or they were carried on stretchers and in wheelbarrows; the blind were led by their companions. It was believed that the nearer an invalid got to the relics, the greater the chance of a cure—so some tried to sleep on the shrine or tomb itself.

All-night vigils in a church housing a shrine could be boisterous affairs. Apart from the cries of the infirm and the shouts of those who thought themselves possessed by demons, there might also be loud uninhibited praying and singing. The *Pilgrim's Guide* describes such a scene in the cathedral of Santiago de Compostela as pilgrims from France, Germany, Italy, and other countries gathered together in groups, holding so many candles aloft that the church seemed to be bathed in daylight. In the general hubbub people wept for their sins or read psalms aloud, some gossiped or ate picnics, while others sang in their native languages, accompanied by lyres, timbrels, flutes, harps, and other instruments.

Sometimes the crowds could get out of hand. In the twelfth century, Abbot Suger of the monastery of St. Denis, near Paris, described how on feast days pilgrims would pack themselves into the monastery church to view the relics of St. Denis. The crowds outside would try to jam themselves in, while those inside were so squashed that they could not move. On occasions panic ensued and pilgrims were crushed underfoot, and it was not unknown for the monastic guardians of the shrine to be forced to take up the relics and scramble to safety through a window.

At St. Peter's in Rome, one of the most important relics was the *sudarium* of St. Veronica (often known simply as the Veronica), the veil believed to have been miraculously imprinted with the features of Jesus after Veronica gave it to him to wipe his face on the way to his execution. When the Veronica was displayed in the Jubilee Year of 1300, such huge crowds surged forward to see it that some were severely injured in the crush. One of the recorded victims was an English pilgrim named William of Derby, whose leg was smashed and who died shortly afterward.

On less crowded occasions, pilgrims could be safely guided around a pilgrimage church by authorized guides who doubtless persuaded them of the spiritual benefit of donating money or other gifts such as rings, brooches, and pins at the principal shrine and the various altars. Pilgrims' offerings were often the mainstay of a shrine's upkeep. They could range from paupers' pennies to a rich man's donation of gold, silver, and gemstones; they could include livestock such as chickens and geese and commodities such as wax, cheese, and oil. In the twelfth century, King Louis VII of France donated an annual gift to the monks of Canterbury of a hundred barrels of wine from his personal cellars, granted in perpetuity.

In addition to leaving donations, pilgrims also left votive offerings, often cast in wax or made of wood or silver, that represented the nature of their illness or condition from which they hoped to be cured (or had been cured) by the intervention of the saint. For example, a man from Montpellier, who had successfully prayed to the Virgin Mary for the recovery of two missing oxen, took two wax miniatures of the beasts to the Church of Our Lady at Rocamadour (in southwest France) as a token of his gratitude. An assortment of votive objects could be seen at shrines, such as crutches and small paintings showing the pilgrims or the miracles they had received. Models of eyes, teeth, arms, and ears—usually on sale outside the shrine—would signify the healing of those particular parts of the body, while a model ship or anchor might betoken being saved from a shipwreck. Another custom was to leave a candle of the same height as the person who needed healing. The thread used to measure the height of the invalid was often made into the candlewick and if the person was very tall it was first wound into a "trindle," or coil, before being set in the wax.

Before leaving the shrine for the journey home, pilgrims might take away holy water which had touched the saint's relics, or dust from his or her tomb; or if they had gone to a shrine for penitential reasons, they would obtain a certificate from a sacristan to prove that they had visited it. Another common practice was purchasing the shrine's "sign," or badge, which was usually made of tin, pewter, brass, or lead and often perforated. Pinned onto hats and cloaks, these badges were not only souvenirs of the journey—like the exotic passport stamps of modern travelers—but also showed that the person in question was a bona fide pilgrim.

The best-known pilgrimage badge was the scallop shell, at first associated only with Santiago de Compostela, but later so popular that it came to signify pilgrimage in general. In the Holy Land pilgrims could buy a palm leaf to take home (the English surname "Palmer" comes from this practice), while in Rome there were two main badges: one showed St. Peter and St. Paul with a key and a sword; the other was the so-called vernicle, a representation of the Veronica that came in the form of either a badge or a small cloth. (In William Langland's *Piers Plowman*, the eponymous pilgrim hero bears on his hat a "hundred small vials" and shell badges from Santiago; he also has the sign of the cross on his cloak, along with a token of the keys of Rome and a vernicle pinned to his chest.) In Amiens (in northern France) badges showed the head of John the Baptist, in Rocamadour the Virgin Mary, and in Cologne the Magi. Canterbury had a number of different signs. Most depicted St. Thomas, whether riding a horse, sitting on his archiepiscopal throne, or standing on board a ship. Another popular Canterbury badge showed the ampulla, the lead flask used by pilgrims to take back "Canterbury water," an efficacious elixir made from water mixed with, allegedly, drops of St. Thomas's blood.

The manufacture and selling of badges was a lucrative business, and monopolies were granted by popes to produce them. In 1199, Innocent III gave the canons of St. Peter's in Rome the sole right to make and sell badges relating to their church; and in 1207 the same pope attempted to stop unauthorized badge-sellers plying their trade in Spain along the road to Santiago. The fact that subsequent popes tried to halt this practice on four more occasions during the thirteenth century indicates that badge-sellers were a determined breed. In Rocamadour, the right to sell badges was shared by the bishop of Tulle and the De Valon family, who also split the profits. Rocamadour locals, watching money for badges change hands rapidly, decided to produce badges themselves—illegally—and for a while significantly cut into the profits of the licensed traders.

Badges were also believed to be receptacles of spiritual power. Pilgrims would press them onto a shrine's holy relics in order to absorb their "spiritual energy," believing this would provide physical protection against malefactors on the return journey. Back home the badges were often fixed to the sides of houses, cattle-sheds, and wells or buried in fields, so that they could work their positive influence. The French king Louis XI (1423–1483) was so convinced of the power of badges that he festooned his hat with them and would kiss them at every opportunity, especially when receiving good or bad news.

10

ROME

"I strongly recommend the wonderful panorama of the whole city. There is so great a forest of towers, and so many palatial buildings, that no one has counted them."

Master Gregory, a medieval English churchman

Rome's enduring importance for Christians was based on two main historical reasons. First, it had more saints and martyrs to honor than any other city. These included the two greatest Christian apostles, St. Peter and St. Paul, who, according to tradition, were executed and laid to rest there. Second, in medieval times the city's ancient status as "mistress of the world" (as Pope Gregory the Great called it) and its grandiose monuments—such as the Forum, Colosseum, and various triumphal arches—still inspired awe, even in their dilapidated state. As the twelfth-century French bishop Hildebert of Lavardin wrote in a poem, "Nothing matches you, O Rome, although you are in ruin / Your broken buildings show how great you were in former times."

Rome's attraction for pilgrims fluctuated according to the ever-shifting prestige of the papacy, along with the level of political stability in Italy. Feuding between rival Italian city-states as well as between pope and Holy Roman emperor frequently led to wars that devastated the countryside and spawned outlaws, robbers, and, in later times, condottieri (mercenary soldiers). An anonymous Rome-bound English pilgrim in the 1300s recorded that there had recently been a war in Italy which had involved no fewer than twelve parties: Milan, Pavia, Piacenza, Cremona, Mantua, Bobbio, Padua, Florence, Bologna, Reggio, Modena, and Pisa.

Physical conditions in Rome itself could also deter pilgrims. In summer it was often unbearably hot, with the threat of malaria. The Welsh chronicler Adam of Usk, who came to Rome in the early 1400s, lamented how what had once been a city of nobles and fine palaces was now a place of robbers, shacks, wolves, and vermin. Nevertheless, even during the 1300s, when the then French-dominated papacy moved from Rome to Avignon in the south of France (a period known as the "Babylonian captivity"), Rome still attracted a steady stream of pilgrims. This was particularly so in the Jubilee Years of 1300, 1350, and 1390, when, as mentioned, plenary indulgences were granted to all those who visited the city and its shrines.

The main attraction for making a pilgrimage to Rome was to gain absolution from sin and thereby smooth the path to heaven in the afterlife—for who could facilitate this better than the city's greatest saint, Peter, the gatekeeper of heaven? Alcuin of York said that people went to Rome "either to mourn their sins [. . .] in the presence of the blessed apostles, or to prepare with more abounding hope to open the way to celestial life." In early medieval times, those who traveled with this hope included bishops, monks, and even monarchs. The latter included, as noted, the Anglo-Saxon Wessex kings Caedwalla and Ine, who is said to have founded the Schola Saxonum, a hostel in Rome specifically for English pilgrims. Hostels were also established by other peoples, including the Franks, Lombards, and Frisians, and these institutions probably evolved into small communities of expatriates, which some pilgrims joined to live out the rest of their lives.

For pilgrims from western Europe there were several main routes to Rome, and they had to negotiate the Alps, which were usually crossed by one of three passes: the Simplon, Mount Cenis, and Great

St. Bernard. Their elevations (up to about 8,000 feet) and freezing temperatures were a constant challenge. Adam of Usk had to blindfold himself as he was borne over the snowy peaks in an ox-wagon. When John of Canterbury, crossing the Great St. Bernard in 1188, reached for his ink-bottle he found the liquid frozen solid. His beard was shaggy with ice and his breath "congealed in a long icicle." But at least he did not freeze to death in the Alps, a fate that befell Aelfsige, archbishop of Canterbury, in 959.

A monk named Nicholas of Munkathvera traveled from Iceland to Rome in the mid-twelfth century. His pilgrimage itinerary gives a good idea of the route pilgrims took from Scandinavia and Germany. After sailing from Iceland to Norway, Nicholas traveled to Denmark, then headed almost due south through Germany. On the way he stopped at Minden, Mainz, Worms, Speyer, and Strasbourg. He proceeded to Basel in Switzerland and from there to the Great St. Bernard Pass, famous for its hospice founded by St. Bernard of Menthon in the eleventh century. Descending from the Alps, Nicholas traveled across the fertile plain of Lombardy via Pavia and Piacenza. The next stop was Lucca, where he could have seen the town's famous Volto Santo, a venerable wooden crucifix said to have protective powers (which could be transferred, so it was believed, to countless facsimiles of it made by local craftsmen). From Lucca he proceeded south, stopping at Siena, Viterbo, and Sutri before entering Rome.

The city offered a dizzying number of churches, shrines, and relics for pilgrims. As early as the fourth century, there had been the *Depositio martyrum*, a list of some of the Christian martyrs of Rome and their burial places; and from the seventh century onward, written guides were describing pilgrimage circuits of the city that included stops at various catacombs, churches, and shrines, climaxing with St. Peter's Basilica. Beginning in the mid-eighth century, the relics of martyrs were transferred from the catacombs outside the city to churches within, thereby increasing the number of churches with sacred objects. By the time Sigeric, archbishop of Canterbury, arrived in Rome in 990 there were at least twenty-three churches to visit, which Sigeric managed to accomplish in two days. Over the course of time, however, seven churches gained precedence over the others. These were the four major basilicas of St. Mary the Greater, St. Paul Outside the Walls, St. John Lateran, and St. Peter, and, in addition, the churches of St. Cross, St. Lawrence, and St. Sebastian. In the later Middle Ages it became necessary to visit all seven to gain a plenary indulgence.

Of the four major basilicas, St. Mary the Greater (Santa Maria Maggiore) on the city's Esquiline Hill drew pilgrims because of its alleged fragments of the True Cross and the Holy Crib. According to legend, the Virgin Mary appeared to Pope Liberius (d. 366) in a vision and told him to build a church at a location that would be indicated miraculously. Then, during the height of summer, a fall of snow dusted the top of the Esquiline, and Liberius drew the outline of the basilica in the snow. (The anniversary of the miracle of the snow is celebrated annually at mass on August 5, when a "snowfall" of white petals is released inside the church.)

St. Paul Outside the Walls was founded by Emperor Constantine and consecrated in 324. It was constructed on a site about one and a half miles south of the city walls (and completely rebuilt in the nineteenth century after a disastrous fire). St. Paul's was the largest church in Rome before St. Peter's was rebuilt in the 1500s; and because it housed the tomb of the apostle Paul, it was always a prime destination for pilgrims. Somewhat isolated from the daily life of the city and without the protection of its walls, the basilica was liable to neglect— as in the eleventh century, when sheep used to wander into the nave. Matters improved in 1070 when a wealthy family from Amalfi presented the church with a pair of magnificent Byzantine bronze doors. The Italian spice merchant William of Ventura recorded that in the Jubilee Year of 1300, so many pilgrims visited St. Paul's that two clerics worked day and night at the high altar to gather in with rakes the mounds of coins left there.

St. John Lateran, the oldest of the major basilicas and the official church of the diocese of Rome, evolved out of a pagan Roman palace complex. It became the papal residence from the fourth century until the early 1300s. According to the twelfth-century guidebook known as *Mirabilia Urbis Romae* ("Wonders of the City of Rome"), pilgrims came to St. John Lateran to see a wide variety of relics, including the Scala Sancta, the holy staircase allegedly taken from the residence of Pontius Pilate and made sacred by Jesus's footsteps; earth retrieved from the tomb of St. John the Evangelist; the rod of Aaron; vials of blood and water from the side of the crucified Christ; and even bits from the five loaves and two fishes with which Jesus fed the multitude. Perhaps the most significant relic was an ancient full-length painting depicting Jesus. Created on wood, the picture was known as the *Acheiropita* (Greek for "not created by human hands") because it was believed to have been made by divine agency. Until the 1500s, the image was taken in procession from St. John Lateran to St. Mary the Greater on the Feast of the Assumption in August.

Rome's greatest church, however, was St. Peter's on Vatican Hill, built in the fourth century by Emperor Constantine over what was believed to be the tomb (or cenotaph) of the apostle. An indication of what early pilgrims did when visiting St. Peter's is given by St. Gregory of Tours, who sent his deacon Agiulf to Rome in about 590 to collect relics. According to Gregory, the apostle's shrine had a small opening through which people poked their heads to make a petition to the saint, while at the same time letting down a *brandeum*, or strip of cloth. If, after it had been withdrawn, the cloth felt heavier than before, it was believed that the prayer had been successful because the *brandeum* had absorbed some of the saint's virtue.

Medieval pilgrims would have been amazed to see St. Peter's as the vast domed Renaissance structure familiar to us today. Until the early 1500s, St. Peter's retained the long rectangular exterior of a traditional Roman basilica, but had evolved inside with the addition of a crypt and various altars and treasures. These included the Veronica, which in the 1300s became St. Peter's main attraction. Visitors were struck even by the old basilica's size and grandeur—an anonymous fourteenth-century English pilgrim commented on the building's "five roofs and four rows of columns" and the fact that it was "as long as a crossbow will shoot." Outside, on the steps leading up to the church, small stalls sold fruit, bread, fish, vegetables, and other foodstuffs.

There was also a range of services on offer, including those of a dentist and a cobbler.

––––––––

Pilgrim traffic to Rome and its myriad churches and shrines was relatively meager during the 1100s, but in the next century the numbers increased. This was partly due to the loss of the Crusader states in the Levant to Muslim armies, which encouraged pilgrims to go elsewhere, but also because Pope Innocent III and his successors improved facilities for pilgrims, created badges to rival those of other shrines, and increased the number of indulgences that could be obtained.

An even greater incentive for pilgrims to go to Rome was a Jubilee Year, or Holy Year. On these occasions pilgrims swelled Rome's native population by tens of thousands. The Christian Jubilee was probably suggested by the Jewish tradition of the "jubilee" year that God tells Moses to institute, as related in Leviticus 25:10 ("Consecrate the fiftieth year and proclaim liberty throughout the land to all its inhabitants. It shall be a jubilee for you; each of you is to return to your family property and to your own clan"). The first Christian Jubilee Year in 1300 was a great success (at least partly due to the plenary indulgences offered), with estimated crowds of between two hundred thousand and two million pilgrims arriving. One witness compared the incoming pilgrims to a swarm of ants or the dense lines of an army. Dante alluded to the crowds in his *Inferno*, as well as to the one-way system enforced on the bridge of Sant' Angelo to ease congestion.

The second Jubilee Year, in 1350, was also a papal triumph—even though Rome had recently suffered from a serious earthquake, and large swaths of Europe were being devastated by the Black Death; plus there was the incessant warfare between England and France. Subsequent Jubilees, held at varying intervals, continued to draw large numbers. The Jubilee in 1450 was the occasion of a tragic accident on the bridge of Sant' Angelo. A panic-stricken mule set off an uproar among the packed pedestrians and scores of people were crushed or drowned in the Tiber. The pilgrims who came to Rome in the Holy Year 1475 (the interval between Jubilees was by this time fixed at twenty-five years) were able to cross a new bridge, the Ponte Sisto, built to siphon off some of the crowds from Sant' Angelo.

———

It is not clear how many pilgrims visited Rome in 1500—the last Jubilee before the Reformation unfolded. But the city they encountered was probably far from what they had imagined. By this time, according to Peter Partner, "Rome was pervaded by rusticity. Cows ruminated in the Forum; horses cropped the grass round the Columns of Trajan and Marcus Aurelius; sheep roamed over at least four of the Seven Hills. The Palatine Hill was covered by vineyards; the Circus Maximus was a market garden. For all its echoes of the Empire of the Caesars, for all the clerical pageantry of its priestly residents, Rome was only a large, medieval village, smelling of cows and hay." And if the city had degenerated structurally, so had the papacy. Pilgrims were probably unaware, by and large, of the corruption of the astute but self-serving Pope Alexander VI (r. 1492–1503), who, as Rodrigo Borgia, had bribed his way to the pontificate. It is difficult to judge whether negative opinions of the papacy tarred Rome's status as a place of pilgrimage with the same brush. Most simple, uneducated pilgrims no doubt arrived in the city, worshipped, prayed, collected their indulgences, bought souvenirs, and left without much knowledge of (or concern for) papal or church corruption. But others did care, and saw Pope Alexander as the epitome of the church's woes and Rome as their epicenter. One of the most vociferous critics was the Florentine reformer Savonarola, who railed against the decadence of the "prostitute church." He was excommunicated by the pope and, after his fellow citizens had become sickened by his extreme morality, executed in Florence in 1498. There were other critics. Erasmus used satire to expose what he saw as church iniquities; and in 1517 the German monk Martin Luther attacked the sale of indulgences, intended by Pope Leo X to raise money to continue the renovation of St. Peter's. While Rome's greatest building awaited fresh funds, the edifice of the church began to tremble as the voices of reform grew louder.

11

SANTIAGO DE COMPOSTELA

*"A weaver in Nantua, a town between Geneva and
Lyons, refused bread to a pilgrim of St. James who
asked for it; and at once he saw his cloth fall to the
ground, ripped apart."*

Pilgrim's Guide (to Santiago de Compostela)

The pilgrimage to the cathedral shrine of Santiago de Compostela in Galicia, northwest Spain—believed to be the home of the relics of St. James (in Spanish, *Santiago*) the Apostle—was the greatest in medieval Christendom after those to Rome and Jerusalem. At the height of its popularity, in the late eleventh and twelfth centuries, an estimated half a million pilgrims a year walked the roads and paths throughout Europe that ultimately led across the Pyrenees and the sun-burned, windswept plains of northern Spain to the misty green mountains of Galicia, and onward to the shrine. Santiago's pilgrim badge was the ubiquitous scallop shell. Dante, in *La Vita Nuova* (c. 1293), defined "pilgrim" in two ways—as someone who had left his place of birth and, more specifically, as someone who had journeyed to Santiago.

How St. James became Spain's national saint and, indeed, how his body supposedly reached Galicia are more the stuff of legend than of fact. Although the seventh-century English monk Aldhelm recorded that St. James had preached in Spain, there is no mention of this in early Christian texts or in the New Testament. What can be gleaned from the Gospels is that James, along with his brother John, was one of Jesus's closest disciples and was termed "the Greater" to distinguish him from another apostle of the same name. Born in Galilee, James and John were the sons of a man named Zebedee and nicknamed "Boanerges" ("Sons of Thunder"), perhaps because of their volcanic tempers.

The New Testament remains mostly silent about James's life after Jesus's crucifixion in about 33 CE, except to note in the Acts of the Apostles (12:2) that he was martyred in Judea in around 44 CE by King Herod Agrippa I. So how did his body come to Galicia, and how did his cult begin? Medieval legends present the answers to these questions in two distinct phases: the first deals with the miraculous transportation and burial of the apostle just after his martyrdom, the second with the equally miraculous discovery of his body hundreds of years later.

According to the thirteenth-century compilation of saints' lives known as *The Golden Legend*, after James's death two of his disciples carried his corpse to Jaffa on the coast of Palestine, where they found a boat "without a rudder or steersman." They nevertheless put out to sea and let God guide the vessel. The boat was duly blown westward through the Pillars of Hercules (the Strait of Gibraltar), then northward to land on the coast of Galicia at the Roman settlement of Iria Flavia. The ruler of that area was a wily pagan queen named Lupa ("She-wolf"), who, after hindering the disciples, finally allowed the apostle's body to be buried in the middle of her palace, which she turned into a church, having accepted the Christian faith herself.

The second phase of the story is set some eight hundred years after James's death. The political circumstances had radically changed. Much of Spain was now dominated by Muslim rulers. In 813, during the reign of Alfonso II, the Christian king of Asturias, a hermit in Galicia was reputedly guided by a celestial light to a field in which he discovered a stone tomb. The local bishop inspected the bones in the tomb, identified them as the remains of St. James, and alerted King Alfonso, who visited the site. Perhaps realizing the potential of such a momentous discovery, the king adopted James as patron saint and had a church built on the burial site. This became known as Compostela (the first written record of the name occurs in a tenth-century document), a word that was popularly thought to derive from the Latin *campus*, "field," and *stella*, "star," in reference to the celestial light that led the hermit to the fateful field. An alternative explanation is that the name comes from the Latin *compostum*, "cemetery," or possibly from *composta*, meaning "established" and referring to the city's first stronghold.

At a time when the Christian reconquest of Spain from its Muslim rulers was in need of momentum, the tenacious faith and moments of aggression that James displays in the Gospel stories made him an ideal patron saint of Santiago de Compostela and of Christian Spain. The saint's symbolic value to the Christian forces is illustrated by his impact on the legendary battle of Clavijo in 844, an event that most scholars believe was an invention of a later medieval writer: the Christian soldiers faced annihilation by a large Muslim army, but when all seemed lost, their king had a vision in which St. James appeared as a knight on a white charger, promising to lead the Christians to victory. The king relayed the vision to his troops, and they were duly inspired and routed the enemy. The story shows how the apostle of the Gospels slipped into a new identity in the medieval Christian Spanish psyche and became a crusading warrior saint: before long he was called Santiago Matamoros, the "Moor Killer," mounted on a horse and wielding a sword.

Especially interesting about the story of St. James's miraculous journey to Spain is how it echoes the Irish *peregrini* and the way they let God guide their journeys across land and sea for the love of Christ. Was the writer of *The Golden Legend* influenced by tales of the early medieval Irish pilgrims, which he combined with other stories that linked James with Spain? The Santiago legend is also reminiscent of the archetypal myth of the "sleeping hero," in which a legendary national figure such as King Arthur or Emperor Frederick I (Barbarossa) defies death and lies sleeping in a hideaway place, ready to wake up when his country needs him.

As news of the rediscovery of the remains of St. James and his efficacy as a divine warrior filtered across Europe, pilgrims began to make their way to Santiago de Compostela in increasing numbers, and thus the Camino de Santiago was born. One of the first documented foreign pilgrims was Godescalc, the bishop of Le Puy in France, who led a group of followers to Spain in about 950. In the next century, Santiago grew more prosperous as the great French monastery of Cluny drew it into its orbit. Perceiving the Spanish shrine and its warrior saint as crucial factors in the fight against Muslim Spain, the Cluniacs built hospices, priories, and bridges to facilitate the passage of pilgrims to Santiago. The city's prestige was further enhanced in 1078 when a new Romanesque cathedral was built, complete with an ambulatory at the east end to enable more pilgrims to walk around the high altar. (The cathedral was completed in the early thirteenth century and given a virtuoso Baroque facade in the 1700s.)

A network of various Santiago routes became established across Europe, and these channeled into four main pilgrim routes in France—starting from Paris (or Tours), Vézelay in Burgundy, Le Puy in the Auvergne, and Arles in Provence—all acting as assembly points for pilgrims. These four routes headed southwest to the Pyrenees, which they traversed via two passes. Once in Spain the paths converged to form one main route known as the *Camino Francés*, the "French Way," which medieval travelers imagined to be reflected at night in the stellar trail of the Milky Way (which they nicknamed the Way of St. James).

Santiago de Compostela's prestige was maintained during the 1100s, largely through the efforts of its dynamic bishop Diego Gelmírez. The popularity of the pilgrimage at this time is shown by the appearance of the *Pilgrim's Guide*, thought to have been partly written by a French monk named Aimery Picaud in about the 1140s. The *Pilgrim's Guide* (which is part of a larger manuscript known as the *Codex Calixtinus*) brings to life the routes and traveling conditions of the Santiago pilgrimage, as well as the various people, customs, food, places to stay, relics, and hazards likely to be encountered during the journey.

Full of insider knowledge, the *Pilgrim's Guide* is both frank and full of prejudices, especially in its description of local peoples. While claiming that the men of the Poitou region in France are handsome, spirited, generous, and make brave, skillful soldiers (not surprisingly, Aimery Picaud was from Poitou), it criticizes the people of Bordeaux for their coarse speech, though their wine is considered excellent, as is their fish. Farther south in France, the Gascons are branded as poor, greedy, garrulous, and having rough manners, tending to drink from the same cup and dressing shabbily; but they are good fighters and hospitable. The Basques are lambasted for speaking a barbarous language and extorting money from pilgrims; and the people of Navarre in Spain are stigmatized as perfidious drunks addicted to robbing and murdering.

The *Pilgrim's Guide* divides the 500-mile route through Spain itself—the Camino—into thirteen stages, starting from the pass of Roncesvalles in the Pyrenees. Yet it would be misleading to see the Camino as one sole route stretching from the Pyrenees to Santiago from which pilgrims did not stray. Although they would have followed the *Camino Francés* for much of the journey, they would also deviate to other paths—perhaps to visit a local shrine, to take a shortcut, to avoid a potential trouble spot, or to make a detour around a broken bridge or flooded road. And many English pilgrims preferred to sail directly to northwest Spain and journey from there along the coast to the shrine.

From Roncesvalles, pilgrims headed southwest to Pamplona; Puente la Reina with its famous pilgrim bridge; and the town of Estella (nestling below a gorge), which, according to the *Pilgrim's Guide*, produced fine wine, fish, meat, and bread. Continuing west to the city of Burgos, they passed through Villafranca, founded (as its name suggests) by French pilgrims in the 1100s. From there the route continued to Léon (established on the site of an ancient Roman legion camp—"Léon" derives from "legion") and to Astorga, a town that had at its medieval height over twenty pilgrim hospices.

By now pilgrims had traveled about two thirds of their Spanish journey, and from this point onward the scenery changed, with mountains looming and the enticing prospect of Galicia beyond. The next significant stop was the village of Foncebadón, lying almost 5,000 feet above sea level, where travelers would add a stone to a cairn. From there the Camino ran down the western slopes of the mountains to Ponferrada, the site of a still-surviving castle taken over by the Knights Templar in the twelfth century, and Villafranca del Bierzo, another town named for French pilgrims. Here, at the local church's Gate of the Pardon, pilgrims who were physically unable to manage the rest of the journey were granted the indulgence they would have received at Santiago.

The next main stage was Palas de Rei—the *Pilgrim's Guide*'s penultimate stop—named for the palace of a Visigothic king. Just before the final approach to Compostela, at the chapel of San Marcos, pilgrims would climb the hill of Monte do Gozo to catch their first glimpse of the cathedral and its soaring towers and to add a stone to the cairn there, thus earning a hundred days off their stint in purgatory.

In Santiago itself, pilgrims made their way to the cathedral square, where they could buy scallop shells and badges and various items of kit, such as shoes, belts, and scrips, as well as medicinal herbs. There, too, they could refresh themselves in the fountain (with its bronze column topped by four lions) spewing water into a basin said to be big enough to hold fifteen people. The crowning act of the pilgrimage was to enter the cathedral's vast interior and seek out the shrine of St. James. The building, the *Pilgrim's Guide* said, measured "fifty-three times the height of a man" in length (about 300 feet), and was filled with stone and white marble columns carved with flowers, birds, animals, humans, and biblical scenes. It had two stories, "like a royal palace," and its upper galleries contained three of the cathedral's fourteen altars. At the east end, three large silver lamps hung in front of the altar of St. James.

After pilgrims had toured the nave, the transepts, and the ambulatory, their devotions reached a climax with the descent into the crypt to touch, kiss, and pray at St. James's tomb. This, according to the

Pilgrim's Guide, was "lit by the otherworldly gleam of carbuncles, honored without cease by heavenly fragrances, bathed in the glow of celestial candles and watched over by attendant angels." Having visited the tomb the pilgrims were, at long last, allowed to receive their indulgence for the pilgrimage. After that they could visit other churches and the rest of the city, before contemplating the long, difficult journey home.

Most pilgrims would return from Santiago de Compostela with a new perspective on life; the *Pilgrim's Guide*, for one, claimed that whoever enters Santiago sad will leave it happy.

12

CANTERBURY

"Gold was the meanest thing to be seen there [. . .]
some [jewels] were larger than the egg of a goose."

Erasmus, describing the
shrine of St. Thomas Becket

When Thomas Becket became archbishop of Canterbury in 1162, during the reign of King Henry II, Canterbury Cathedral was the spiritual center of English Christianity, as it had been since the time of the missionary saint Augustine at the end of the sixth century. It was not yet known as a pilgrimage place. But after Becket's assassination by four of Henry's knights on December 29, 1170, and his canonization in 1173, Canterbury became one of the major pilgrim destinations of medieval Christendom, alongside Santiago de Compostela, Rome, and Jerusalem. For 350 years, until the Reformation, pilgrims converged on the cathedral "from every shire's end of England," as Chaucer wrote, and from all over continental Europe.

Canterbury's birth, growth, decline, and temporary end as a place of pilgrimage are relatively well defined and documented, beginning with Becket's martyrdom and ending with the Protestant reformers' destruction of the shrine in the 1500s. At the same time it also attracted its fair share of pious legends. Medieval reports claimed that St. Thomas appeared in visions and that through him the blind saw, the deaf heard, and the crooked were made straight. As mentioned, drops of what was said to be his blood were added to the cathedral's well to produce a unique elixir with which pilgrims eagerly filled their ampullas, or lead flasks. Emperors and kings paid homage to the saint, including Henry II himself, who, in 1174, walked barefoot to the shrine in a public show of penitence and allowed himself to be symbolically scourged by the monks there. Even Henry VIII prayed at the shrine only a few years before his self-serving state policies resulted in the shrine's destruction in 1538.

St. Thomas's shrine in the cathedral not only radiated spiritual power but also possessed great material wealth, from the coins donated by peasants to the gold and silver plates, cups, brooches, and gems offered by the wealthy. Most spectacular, perhaps, was the gift of the French king Louis VII, who in 1179 presented an enormous ruby— *le Régale de France*—which was fated to end up in one of Henry VIII's rings. When Henry's men hauled off the shrine's wealth they needed twenty-six wagons to carry out the task.

Canterbury is inextricably tied up with the life of Becket, who as Henry II's chancellor had upheld the power of the state against the church, but then, as archbishop, became the implacable defender of ecclesiastical rights; originally a man of the world, fastidious in his choice of food and wine, he became an austere churchman reveling in asceticism: when the Canterbury monks examined his dead body, they found beneath his robes a hair shirt seething with lice. Despite justified charges of pride, obstinacy, and ostentation, Becket still emerges as a rock of principle from the swirling waters of corruption in twelfth-century church and state politics. His willpower, self-conviction, and loyalty—whether to the king or, subsequently, to the church—as well as his dignity and charisma made him popular with the common people, but also a marked man among envious fellow clerics and avaricious nobles.

Becket was born in London in about 1118, the son of a wealthy

Anglo-Norman merchant. In his mid-twenties he joined the household of Theobald, archbishop of Canterbury, who was so impressed by his charm, energy, and all-round competence that he had no hesitation in recommending him to Henry II for the post of chancellor, one of the most important positions in the country. Not only did Becket perform his new duties with zest, he also formed a close friendship with the king, to the extent that Theobald remarked in a letter to Becket that, in popular opinion, "you and the king are one heart and one mind."

When Theobald died in 1161, King Henry must have seen a heaven-sent opportunity to appoint Becket as the new archbishop of Canterbury—and through him to wield greater influence over the church. For some time the relationship between crown and church had been vexed, with both parties seeking to extend or consolidate their spheres of interest, which were often mutually exclusive. One major sticking point was the right of the church to try churchmen charged with breaking the law in ecclesiastical courts—where punishments were relatively lenient—and not in civil courts. Henry, a headstrong man prone to violent fits of temper, was determined to bring the church to heel on this and other matters; and now he had the chance to install his own man, his boon companion, at the top of the clerical pyramid.

Despite Becket's reluctance and forebodings, in 1162 Henry had him ordained a priest, consecrated as a bishop, and enthroned as archbishop in the space of thirty-six hours. But any sense of triumphal expectation Henry might have had soon drained away as he watched Becket transfer his immense talents and loyalty to another, heavenly, master—and take up the church's cause. The king and archbishop, equally matched, made moves and countermoves like chess grandmasters, each trying to rally support, exert pressure, and gain advantage for his cause. Then, in 1164, feeling the full force of the king's frustrated anger, Becket decided it would be prudent to flee to France. There he remained until 1170, when a partial rapprochement with Henry enabled him to return to England and a hero's welcome from the common people. But the modicum of renewed goodwill between the two men evaporated when Becket openly denounced the two bishops who, during his exile, had officiated at the crowning of Henry's young son as coregent—contrary to canon law.

When news of Becket's latest defiance reached Henry, on campaign in France, he is said to have shouted, "Will no one rid me of this lowborn priest?" The question may have been rhetorical—but four of Henry's knights took him at his word. On reaching Canterbury they forced a confrontation with Becket, who, realizing their intention and seemingly resigned to martyrdom, refused to flee or to admit their charges of treason. Cajoled by his fretting monks to take refuge, Becket retreated to the cathedral but refused to let them bar the door, declaring that they should not make "a fortress of the house of God; by suffering rather than by fighting we shall triumph over the enemy." The four knights followed him and, careless of the sanctity of the place, struggled with the archbishop and cut him down, slicing off a piece of his skull in the process. They then raided the archbishop's palace for valuables and rode off into the night.

While Christendom reacted with shock and outrage to what Pope Alexander III called "this most monstrous crime," and King Henry received the news of his erstwhile friend's death with what appeared to be genuine grief, the cult of Thomas Becket was born. The first "miracle" had happened on the night after the murder, when a local knight claimed to have cured his paralyzed wife with a cloth he had dipped into Becket's spilt blood. A few days later a Gloucester woman declared she had been cured of severe headaches after praying to Becket, and a Berkshire knight attributed to Becket's intercession the cure of his damaged arm. Other alleged miracles quickly followed, and during the first decade after Becket's death more than seven hundred were recorded by two contemporary monks, Benedict and William. On February 21, 1173, the pope canonized Becket.

At first the saint's tomb lay in the crypt of the cathedral and consisted of a coffin enclosed by a rectangular marble chest. This had two holes on each side to enable pilgrims to reach in and touch the coffin itself. On one occasion an agile madman squeezed himself through one of these holes into the space between the chest and the coffin and managed to scramble out just as the monks were contemplating having to smash the tomb to liberate him.

Pilgrims made their way to the tomb after visiting the spot in the northwest transept where Becket had died, as well as the high altar, where his body had been laid out immediately after his death. In 1220, forty-six years after a fire destroyed part of the cathedral, the saint's remains were ceremonially moved to the newly completed Trinity Chapel and placed inside a gold-plated tomb. Hanging above it was a gold-wire net on which pilgrims left gifts of devotion. East of the tomb lay the Corona Chapel, built to house the severed fragment of Becket's skull, mounted in gold and set with jewels.

Also in the early thirteenth century, some of the miracles were depicted in the cathedral's stained-glass windows. They show, for example, how a workman, accidentally buried alive while laying drainage pipes, was extricated from the ground; and how a monk was cured of skin disease, a forester of an arrow wound, and a carpenter of a leg injury. News of such miracles spread through Europe, as did relics of Becket, including pieces of his clothing and vestments, and domestic utensils. Hymns and commemorative services in his honor echoed around countless churches across the continent, and murals, stained-glass windows, carved roof bosses, and medals were made depicting his final moments.

Apart from the great kings who made their way to Becket's shrine, the most famous pilgrims were probably the fictional characters of Geoffrey Chaucer, whose *Canterbury Tales* describes the journey of a group of pilgrims from London to Canterbury and the tales they recount to entertain each other along the way. Chaucer's characters give a good idea of the types of people who would have trekked to Canterbury in the later Middle Ages—a journey Chaucer himself probably made in 1386. They include a "very perfect, gentle" knight; an urbane monk with a penchant for hunting, whose horse's bridle tinkled with tiny "Canterbury bells"; a poor parson who was "rich in holy thought and work"; a red-bearded miller who played the bagpipes; and the five-times-married Wife of Bath, who was something of a pilgrimage addict, having gone to Jerusalem three times as well as to Rome, Boulogne, Santiago de Compostela, and Cologne.

Setting out from Southwark, pilgrims from London such as Chaucer's group would have traveled southeast along Watling Street to Greenwich, Dartford, and then Rochester, where many visited the tomb of St. William of Perth, a Scottish pilgrim who had been murdered near the town en route to the Holy Land. Farther on lay Sittingbourne, Faversham (where a Cluniac abbey housed a sliver of the True Cross), Boughton, and Harbledown, where the Norman church of St. Nicholas kept part of Becket's shoe, which pilgrims were allowed to kiss. Just beyond Harbledown came the first glimpse of Canterbury Cathedral's two eleventh-century towers on its western facade—they "seem to salute the visitor from afar," Erasmus noted in 1514. Inside the city, the poorer pilgrims would have sought out lodgings at monastic guest houses, while the wealthy resorted to inns and hostelries such as The Chequers, which still survives in its later Tudor incarnation. They would then make their way to the cathedral to be guided around the pilgrimage stations by the resident monks.

The other main pilgrimage route to Canterbury was from Winchester, the principal assembly point for foreigners arriving at the port of Southampton. From Winchester, having visited the cathedral's shrine of St. Swithun, pilgrims headed east, probably by way of Alton, Dorking, and Aylesford, where some would have rested at the Carmelite friary, founded by St. Simon Stock in the twelfth century. Farther east at Boxley they could have seen the famous Boxley Rood, or Crucifix. This wooden statue, which may have been originally designed for pageants, had a hidden mechanism that made its eyes and lips move—in the sixteenth century, the Protestant reformers were to claim that the statue reacted appropriately to the pilgrims' offerings: mere silver made it look vexed but gold apparently caused its "jaws to wag merrily." (The reformers also exposed its "engines and old wire" and eventually burnt it in public.) From Boxley the route passed through Charing, where the relic of John the Baptist's execution block could be seen in the local church, to the village of Chilham and from there beside the River Stour through woods to Canterbury.

Becket's shrine attracted a continual (although in later times diminishing) stream of pilgrims until the early sixteenth century. In 1220 more than £1,100 had been gathered at the shrine; by contrast, in 1535, three years before its destruction, the total was only £36. The drop in income was at least partly due to the late medieval trend that saw centuries-old saints replaced in people's affections by more recent ones. This tendency was reflected in miracle stories such as the one that promoted the claims of the "saintly King Henry VI"—who was murdered in 1471 and came to be viewed as a saint shortly afterward—over those of Becket: allegedly a baby who had swallowed a badge depicting the saint was nearly choking to death until the name of Henry VI was invoked and the badge was duly regurgitated. So Becket was already yesterday's saint when Henry VIII violated his shrine and ordered him to be regarded as a "rebel and traitor," rather than as Chaucer's "holy blissful martyr." Yet though the king tried hard to extirpate Becket's cult—he ordered references to his name in prayer books to be excised and depictions of him in murals and windows obliterated—he could not sever the saint's association with the cathedral any more than he could erase his memory.

13

JERUSALEM AND
THE HOLY LAND

*"How shall we sing the Lord's song in a strange land?
If I forget thee, O Jerusalem, let my right hand
forget her cunning."*

Psalm 137:4–5

"I cared never for eating, drinking, nor sleeping; the hours of darkness which are appointed for men's rest were grievous to me; my bed was a thorn to me, my berth a hell. I could no longer read or write, or converse with men as before; but my only pleasure was to sit at the prow of the galley upon the horns thereof, and from thence to look ceaselessly across the wide sea, that by the toil of my eyes I might quiet the fever of my mind." These words of Felix Fabri, having made two pilgrimages to Jerusalem in the 1480s, convey the intense emotion medieval pilgrims felt waiting for their first glimpse of the Holy Land on the horizon. Ever since Emperor Constantine's mother, Helena, had allegedly located Jesus's tomb and the True Cross, Christian pilgrims had trekked to Palestine, viewing it as the most prized of destinations—the land of Jesus's birth, mission, death, and resurrection.

With the conquests of the Crusaders from the end of the eleventh century, pilgrim traffic to the Holy Land received a new lease on life. But the Crusades eventually petered out and Muslim armies regained their hold of Palestine; the last Crusader stronghold fell in 1291. Even so, Christian pilgrims still journeyed there, but increasingly by sea, as the overland route steadily became more perilous. This was due to political turbulence in eastern Europe and the Byzantine Empire, which was threatened by the Ottoman Turks, who eventually captured Constantinople in 1453.

The most convenient way to travel to the Holy Land in the later Middle Ages was in a Venetian ship. In the early thirteenth century, Venice had developed the first pilgrim "package tours," with private shipowners, licensed by the state, providing transport, food, and accommodation for a payment that also included local taxes and guides' fees. The state reserved the right to inspect ships and impose regulations for the comfort and safety of passengers; this, however, did not stop unscrupulous Venetian captains from sometimes packing in too many pilgrims, or cramming them in by overfilling their ships with cargo on return trips. Another factor in favor of Venetian vessels was that in the 1400s, when hostile Turkish and pirate ships roved around the eastern Mediterranean, Venetian navy patrols provided a degree of security.

One interesting aspect of Felix Fabri's colorful accounts of his two pilgrimages is that he combines a traditional medieval piety with a fresh, humanistic curiosity about the world around him. Through his words it is possible to experience both the interior life of the pilgrim and the novel sights and sounds of the journey. Although devout himself, Fabri is able to distance himself from, and reflect upon, the more extreme expressions of pilgrim devotion and unquestioning belief in miracles that had been commonly found in earlier times. He does not deny the truth of miracle stories, but he prefers a natural explanation if one exists. In the Church of the Holy Sepulchre, for example, he remarks upon six constantly dripping marble columns and mentions the popular tradition that the drops were the columns' "tears," shed in sympathy with Jesus and the Virgin Mary. While acknowledging his respect for the "opinion of the common people," Fabri gives his own considered observation that the dripping is caused by a type of marble so cold that it condenses the air around it into water.

Fabri's first expedition to Palestine, in 1480, proved unsatisfactory, mainly because the Venetian captain in charge of the trip cut it short, leaving his charges only nine frenzied days in which to see the sights of Jerusalem—meager rations after six weeks at sea. As soon as Fabri arrived back in Ulm he vowed to return to the Holy Land. In 1483 he fulfilled his oath, making the journey as a chaplain to four German noblemen. On June 1 their Venetian ship, with its crew, galley slaves, and a motley group of pilgrims from France, Germany, England, Ireland, Hungary, Bohemia, and elsewhere, set off to sea. After stops at Rovigno (Rovinj) on the Croatian coast and Methoni in southwest Greece, they arrived on the island of Crete, where the only available accommodation was a brothel. Luckily, the German proprietress, sensitive to the pilgrims' feelings, cleared the place and provided them with a delicious supper. From Crete the route took them to the islands of Rhodes and Cyprus, after which the pilgrims' anticipation of catching the first glimpse of their destination intensified. Finally, at sunrise on July 1, the Holy Land was sighted—a moment celebrated by a joyful rendering of the *Te Deum*.

The pilgrims' excitement at arriving at Jaffa was soon checked by their reception by the local Muslims, who laboriously registered the new arrivals, then lodged them in some nearby ruined vaults until arrangements for their transfer to Jerusalem could be finalized. Eventually, on July 8, the Muslims provided the pilgrims with donkeys. Fabri employed the same friendly guide whom he had used on his first trip, and gave the man a pair of German iron stirrups, to his evident joy. Escorted by a Muslim bodyguard to protect them from opportunist bedouin tribesmen, the pilgrims set off toward Jerusalem via the town of Ramle, where Father Paul, the prior of the Franciscan house in Jerusalem and chief representative of the Latin Church in Palestine, spelled out for them twenty-seven essential rules the pilgrims had to obey to stay out of trouble with their Muslim hosts. Formulated after years of practical experience, the rules included not stepping over Muslim graves, not laughing aloud in public, not gazing at Muslim women, not entering mosques, and not retaliating to any provocation. Forewarned and forearmed, the group continued on their way until suddenly "like a flash of lightning [. . .] Jerusalem shone forth." Straightaway the pilgrims dismounted and bowed down to the earth and prayed. Then, with "eyes full of tears" and "cheeks wet with joy," they resumed their journey, with the priests and monks singing the *Te Deum*, but softly, so as not to rile the Muslim escort.

The pilgrims entered the city by the Fish Gate and made their way to—but did not yet enter—the Church of the Holy Sepulchre, which, one of the resident friars announced, was "worshipped by the whole world." At these words the pilgrims cast themselves down to kiss the ground and pray, and many were overcome with emotion: some wandered around beating their chests; some sat down and sobbed violently; some lay prostrate, as still as corpses; and some of the women pilgrims "shrieked as though in labor."

The pilgrims were then led off to their lodgings. As a friar, Fabri was allowed to stay in the Franciscan convent on Mount Sion, in the south of the city, while the laymen went to the partially ruined Hospital of St. John. Once settled in and officially welcomed by the Franciscans, the pilgrims began their hectic round of sightseeing. There was no shortage of holy places—almost every prominent rock, gnarled old olive tree, or mysterious ruin seems to have had some alleged association with a biblical event. Fabri mentioned visiting a stone where Peter stood after denying Jesus for the third time; the corner of a house where the Virgin Mary waited while Jesus was being tried; the house where James, patron saint of Santiago de Compostela, was beheaded by Herod Agrippa; the stone that marked where the resurrected Christ greeted the three Marys—and various other sites.

The climax to the sightseeing was undoubtedly a visit to the interior of the Church of the Holy Sepulchre. After the Muslim wardens had let them in, the pilgrims formally processed around inside the church, paying devotions at the numerous holy places. All the while they held candles—Fabri noted with disapproval that some pilgrims felt superior for having candles "curiously twisted and decorated with gilding and painting"—and sang hymns, kissed relics, and collected indulgences. The procession ended at the site of the tomb of Jesus, after which the pilgrims sat in various corners of the church and ate a meal. Later on, at midnight, mass was celebrated—at which overzealous priests competed in an unseemly fashion to conduct the service at the high altar. The following morning the pilgrims were ejected by the Muslims.

So ended the first visit to the Church of the Holy Sepulchre. The pilgrims would return two more times. On the third occasion, the night before most of the pilgrims were departing for home, Fabri recorded that the atmosphere was spoiled by a combination of a plague of fleas, a group of Syrian Christians who were banging pieces of metal as part of their ritual, and the fact that rather than worship and pray, many pilgrims slept, ate, and gossiped. They even, contrary to Father Paul's strict instructions, scratched their names on the holy stonework.

As well as the sights in Jerusalem, there was plenty to see outside the city. One of the highlights was Bethlehem. Braving a group of bedouins who roughly manhandled them outside the town (one of them charged Fabri with a lance and speared his hat), the pilgrims proceeded to the recently refurbished Church of the Holy Nativity. Beneath the choir stood a white marble manger on a marble pavement, and Fabri registered his unease at the disparity between the sumptuousness of the shrine and what must have been the humble simplicity of the original stable. The pilgrims were also shown the cave in which the bodies of the children slain by Herod the Great supposedly had been thrown, and one or two of the pilgrims had a quick look for a relic to take back home.

Another highlight was a two-day excursion to the Jordan River. Some pilgrims plunged in fully dressed to endow their clothing with good fortune; some draped wool and linen in the river, with a view to making garments from the blessed material; others filled bottles and flasks or dipped small bells into the water. Fabri kept cool by sitting in the river, the water up to his neck, taking in the scene.

Officially the pilgrimage ended on July 22, although a few people stayed on to visit Sinai and Egypt, including Fabri, who later sailed home from Alexandria. It is possible, however, to get an idea of the return journey from Jerusalem to Venice from Fabri's account of his first homeward voyage in 1480. That journey had turned out to be a nightmare. The ship carrying the pilgrims, most of whom were exhausted from their whirlwind tour and suffering from sickness, sailed from Jaffa to Cyprus, then made for Rhodes and Crete. Food consisted of tainted meat, stale bread, and worm-riddled biscuit, while water ran seriously short, and the pilgrims were forced to buy discolored water from the crew for more than the price of wine. The sheep, goats, mules, and pigs on board were deprived of water rations and pathetically licked the deck for any moisture.

At Rhodes the pilgrims witnessed the ghoulish aftermath of a failed Turkish siege; corpses littered the seashore, and the city walls and towers were reduced to rubble. On Crete the cheap prices and delicious Malvoisie wine provided some respite, but then came a terrifying storm, with lightning, fierce winds, and mountainous waves. While most of the pilgrims prayed aloud, and some vowed to go on pilgrimage to Rome or Santiago if only they might escape, Fabri himself could not help but think of the words of the ancient sage Anacharsis, "who said that those who are at sea cannot be counted among either the living or the dead [. . .] they were only removed from death by the space of four fingers, four fingers being the thickness of the sides of a ship. Also, when asked which ships were the safest, he replied: 'Those which lie on dry ground, and not in the sea.'" No doubt Fabri also prayed to God and the saints; but his response to the storm again indicates a mind in tune with the humanism of his day, with its delight in classical erudition.

The voyagers survived the storm and made their way up the Adriatic, past Dubrovnik to Porec and from there to Venice. Fabri must have voiced the feelings of all medieval travelers to the Holy Land, and possibly of pilgrims everywhere, when he declared at the end of the account of his first voyage to Palestine, "It requires courage and audacity to attempt this pilgrimage. That many are prompted to it by sinful rashness and idle curiosity cannot be doubted; but to reach the holy places and to return to one's home active and well is the especial gift of God."

14

CHANGING ATTITUDES

*"And when they came to Mount of Calvary she
dropped to the ground, unable to stand or kneel,
but [. . .] spreading her arms out, she shouted as
though her heart would burst."*

Margery Kempe, *Book of Margery Kempe*

The Late Middle Ages—roughly from the fourteenth century
to the beginning of the sixteenth—saw profound changes in
European society that affected the lives and attitudes of all classes,
influencing their perspective on religion, the church, and religious
observances such as pilgrimage. Perhaps the single most dramatic
agent of change was the Black Death, the plague that, from 1347
to 1351, claimed the lives of perhaps over twenty million people
throughout the continent, approximately one third of the total population. The plague had a range of effects, creating tensions in the
fabric of society. In devastated villages, surviving peasant workers suddenly found they were in great demand and could exert leverage for
better pay and working conditions. The denial of these improvements
by government authorities led to increased social tension and, in some
places, violent civil unrest. In 1358, French peasants, suffering from

the effects of the plague, the protracted war with England, and other grievances, rose up against their feudal masters; and in England in 1381, a peasant army converged on London demanding radical social and economic reforms. Both revolts were crushed, but the underlying problems and pressure for change remained.

Meanwhile, the prestige of the church was steadily diminishing. In 1303 the papacy's standing was undermined when a councillor of King Philip IV of France, reacting to Pope Boniface VIII and his assertions of authority, attempted to capture him. Although the capture failed in the end, the fact that someone had dared to assault the leader of Christendom dimmed the aura of papal supremacy. Then, in 1309, the French pope Clement V, under pressure from his king, moved the papal residence to Avignon in the south of France. The papacy's "Babylonian captivity," which lasted for nearly seventy years, drained power away from Rome and caused strong divisions in Europe. Although the papacy eventually returned to the Eternal City in 1377, the following year saw more trouble arise: two men were elected as rival popes, one in Rome, the other back in Avignon, each supported by regional factions. It was the start of the Great Schism. In 1409 a church council (in Pisa) tried to depose the two popes and elect a third, but this ended with the farcical situation of three popes claiming to be the true pontiff. A few years later, the predicament was finally resolved at the Council of Constance, with the election of Martin V as sole pope. But the protracted and unedifying feuding, compromises, and corruption had left their stain on the papacy.

One of those who voiced his outrage against the church and the papacy publicly was the radical English theologian John Wycliffe (c. 1330–1384), who believed that the word of God as manifested in the Bible was the only true authority for Christians. Wycliffe attacked clerical wealth and property ownership and also, more heretically, denied the doctrine of transubstantiation—the belief that the substance of bread and wine changes into the substance of the body and blood of Christ when consecrated in the mass. He saw the host as nothing more than "an effectual sign."

Wycliffe's followers, known as Lollards, continued to promulgate his ideas after his death, even producing an English translation of the Bible in the 1390s, since they believed that the Bible should be read by everyone and not remain a preserve of the priesthood. But in 1401 Henry IV introduced severe measures to stamp out Lollardy, and some years later the movement lost further momentum after a failed uprising led by the Lollard leader Sir John Oldcastle in 1414.

With their condemnation of church practices and hierarchy and their deep suspicion of enjoyment, the Lollards were, not surprisingly, critical of pilgrimage. This is shown in a contemporary account by a man named William Thorpe, who seems to have been a Lollard priest. He described his interrogation for heresy by Thomas Arundel, archbishop of Canterbury, in 1407. When asked who he thought a "true pilgrim" was, Thorpe said it was someone who travels "toward the bliss of heaven" by eschewing evil and embracing the Christian virtues and obeying God's commandments. By contrast, Thorpe condemned those pilgrims who were ignorant of their faith but nevertheless set off on journeys "more for the health of their bodies than of their souls! More to have richesse and prosperity of this world, than for to be enriched with virtues in their souls." These so-called pilgrims, he continued, spent their money in dubious foreign hostelries when they could be spending it at home, helping the poor.

Of course, Thorpe's view that true pilgrimage depended on personal virtue and inner godliness—and not just journeying to some shrine—had been reiterated from the time of the Church Fathers. In the fourth century, St. John Chrysostom had said there was no necessity to make long journeys and that people should pray to God at home. Even St. Jerome, who had done so much to encourage pilgrimage, wrote that God could not be tied to one particular place on earth and that the "court of heaven lies open to Britain and Jerusalem alike." Closer to Thorpe's time, William Langland emphasized in *Piers Plowman* that pilgrims to Rome or Santiago were not necessarily seeking truth: the road to truth involved the practice of Christian virtues.

So marked was the Lollard antagonism to pilgrimage that to go on one—or swear to their validity—was taken as evidence of non-involvement in the heretical movement. A Lollard named William

Dynet, for example, renounced the error of his ways by swearing he would support the cult of saints and would "nevermore despyse pylgremage." Yet going on pilgrimage did not save Margery Kempe from charges of Lollardy and threats of burning.

Born in about 1373 in Lynn, Norfolk, Margery married John Kempe in 1393 and they proceeded to have fourteen children. When she was about forty, she took a vow of chastity and began to go on a number of pilgrimages—to Canterbury, Jerusalem, Rome, Santiago de Compostela, and other smaller shrines. She has been compared to Chaucer's Wife of Bath, a cheerful worldly soul, who had also been to Christendom's major shrines—but Margery Kempe was anything but worldly: her continual visions of Jesus and the saints, and her propensity for "great weeping and boisterous sobbing" in public places, attracted constant bewilderment, scorn, and rejection.

In Venice, for example, to where she had traveled with a company of fellow pilgrims, "her countrymen forsook her and went away from her, leaving her alone. And some of them said that they would not go with her for a hundred pound." Apart from her uninhibited display of emotions, Kempe also provoked hostility by her outspoken criticism of the clergy. Nevertheless, although sometimes hampered by the church authorities, she was still able to carry out her spiritual journeys and, along with insults and threats, she received much goodwill, charity, and fellowship along the way, as her autobiographical *Book of Margery Kempe* describes.

If in later medieval times pilgrimages were losing some of their spiritual rigor, as the criticisms of the Lollards and the tales of Chaucer imply, they were only following a general social trend in which, for example, the increase of commerce and the growth of universities reflected and stimulated a heightened interest in the external world and knowledge for its own sake, not solely for the sake of God. This humanistic curiosity in the world can be discerned in some late medieval pilgrim guidebooks and pilgrims' accounts (such as Felix Fabri's), which delight in details of foreign dress, customs, and language in a way that seems inconceivable in pilgrim itineraries of the first millennium.

One of the strangest late medieval pilgrim accounts was the *Travels of Sir John Mandeville*, which, as Jonathan Sumption has noted, "was the first really popular book to portray travel as an adventure and a romance." First published in about 1357 in French, the *Travels* was purportedly written by an English knight from the town of St. Albans who set off on pilgrimage to the Holy Land in 1322 and then made his way to the lands of the East, which he describes with a keen eye for the exotic. In fact most scholars believe that the book is mainly a compilation of accounts by other travelers and that the author was possibly a citizen of Liège named Jean d'Outremeuse.

Among the scenes the author of the *Travels* describes are the pyramids of Egypt, which he calls the "granaries of Joseph," dismissing the idea that they are "sepulchres of great lords." At the Dead Sea he tells of apple trees whose fruit contains coal and cinders; in Ethiopia there are people who have only one leg with one large foot, with which they shade themselves when lying down; and in India "men worship the ox" and "women shave their beards, and the men not." He also tells of the realms of the powerful emperor of China; of Prester John, a mysterious legendary figure who was rumored to have founded a Christian kingdom somewhere in Asia; and of the terrestrial Paradise—though he admits he has never been there himself.

In a world in which the momentum for exploration and discovery was gathering pace, the *Travels*, filled with facts, fables, and legends, became one of the most popular books of the age and was translated into English, Latin, German, and various other languages. The author himself seemed to sum up the spirit of the times when he referred to the fact that in his day "many men have great liking to hear speak of strange things of diverse countries."

It was this curiosity for the larger world that informed the spirit of the Renaissance and also, for many, undermined the devotional journey. St. Augustine had railed against the effects of *curiositas* in his *Confessions*, stating that people gaze in wonder at mountains, huge waves, wide rivers, the great ocean, or the stars in the sky but "pay no attention to themselves [. . .] For when our hearts become repositories piled high with such worthless stock as this, it is the cause of interruption and distraction from our prayers." It was a sentiment that found a powerful contemporary voice in the late medieval mystic Thomas à Kempis, the likely author of *The Imitation of Christ*. Here we read that people who visited pilgrimage places were "often moved by curiosity and the urge for sight-seeing, and one seldom hears that any amendment of life results, especially as their conversation is trivial and lacks true contrition." A late medieval pilgrim such as Felix Fabri certainly had humanistic curiosity, but it was still underpinned by a deep religious sensibility. Once this religious quality came to be eroded by skepticism and scientific reason, the "pilgrim" became curious about places and objects for the sake of knowledge or for self-improvement.

Pilgrimage was entering the modern age with its different types of travelers, including the "explorer," "merchant," "migrant," and "tourist."

15

FROM REFORMATION
TO ROMANTICISM

*"All pilgrimages should be stopped. There is no
good in them: no commandment enjoins them, no
obedience attaches to them."*

Martin Luther, *Address to the Christian Nobility*

In about 1512 and 1514, Erasmus made pilgrimages to Walsingham and Canterbury, the two preeminent shrines in England, and
later drew on his experiences there when he lampooned aspects of
pilgrimage in an essay entitled "The Religious Pilgrimage" (in his
Colloquies). Such was the power of his pen that some contemporar-
ies believed his writings were partly responsible for the drop in the
numbers of aristocratic pilgrims traveling to the Holy Land, where
the latest regional power, the Ottoman Turks, was making pilgrimage
difficult. Certainly, when St. Ignatius Loyola visited Palestine in 1523
he found few signs of pilgrim activity.

Although dissenting voices had been raised against pilgrimage
before the Reformation, attacks by Erasmus as well as by the Protestant reformers on what they considered to be unscriptural rituals

and "superstition" now took their toll. In 1550 a Spanish church-man named Francisco Molina complained that although more pilgrims were going to Santiago de Compostela than to Rome, "since the damned doctrines of Luther arose, the number of pilgrims has fallen off, and especially from Germany and the wealthy from England."

The Protestant Reformation was not, of course, a preplanned, unified movement masterminded by the German monk Martin Luther (1483–1546). His initial intention had been to correct abuses within the church, not to break away from it. In the end, despite efforts to effect a reconciliation, disagreements between Luther's followers and the church, especially on issues such as clerical marriage and the authority of the pope, proved decisive. Erasmus himself, while critical of the church, still retained his traditional Catholic piety; and his innately peace-loving, scholarly personality shied away from the radicals and militants among the reformers.

Erasmus's "The Religious Pilgrimage," therefore, is the more interesting for being the product of an independent mind. It takes the form of a dialogue between two opposite characters: the skeptical Menedemus and his friend Ogygius, a devout, somewhat naive believer, who has been on pilgrimage to Santiago, Walsingham, and Canterbury. When asked how he found "the good man of St. James" at Santiago, Ogygius replies that the saint has had fewer visits than before because of the "new opinion" that has spread throughout the world: instead of glittering with gold and jewels, St. James has been reduced to the "very block that he is made of," with barely a tallow candle to boast about. Menedemus surmises that if this is true, then the rest of the saints must be in jeopardy, too.

Ogygius next describes his visit to Walsingham, "the holiest name" in England, where, in a chapel "full of marvels," a verger showed him and his companions the giant-sized middle joint of a man's finger claimed to be from the hand of St. Peter. The most precious relic, however, was a vial of milk from the Virgin Mary; when Ogygius dared to ask the verger for evidence of the milk's authenticity the man looked at them "with astonished eyes and a sort of horror" and would have ejected them all as heretics but for a tip.

At Canterbury, Ogygius and a companion (identifiable as Erasmus's friend John Colet, dean of St. Paul's Cathedral) were shown "a world of bones [. . .] skulls, chins, teeth, hands, fingers, whole arms, all of which we kissed." Having gazed at a stockpile of precious ornaments and jewels, the companion told their guide that it would be better to use some of the riches to help the poor; the guide began to "frown and to pout out his lips, and to look upon us as he would have eaten us up." This concern for the poor is echoed by Menedemus (representing the voice of Erasmus himself), who says that although there should be some vestments and vessels to dignify a church, the profusion of golden tombs, candlesticks, and images was an extravagance when "our brothers and sisters [. . .] are ready to die from hunger and thirst."

The social argument against the church's wealth, pomp, and pride—and by association against such activities as processions and pilgrimages—had surfaced throughout the history of Christianity; and now it found powerful new expression through Luther and the Protestant reformers. Born in Eisleben (Saxony-Anhalt) in 1483 to humble parents, Luther became an Augustinian monk and, later, a professor of theology at the University of Wittenberg, newly established by Frederick III, elector of Saxony. In 1515 he started working on a series of lectures on St. Paul's Letter to the Romans, a text that convinced him that people could not save themselves by doing good works (including going on pilgrimage) but only by receiving the grace of God—by being "justified" by their faith.

At the same time, Luther was increasingly concerned about the lax behavior of the clergy, their lack of spirituality, and their concern for their own temporal advancement. Matters came to a head over the sale of indulgences. When a Dominican friar named Johann Tetzel began selling indulgences near Wittenberg to raise money for the debt-ridden Archbishop Albert of Mainz and for Pope Leo X's building program, Luther reacted by circulating his famous Ninety-Five Theses—attacking indulgences and inviting debate about them—in the fall of 1517.

Cutting to the heart of the church's teaching on relics and purgatory, and undermining its authority, Luther's aggressive public challenge could not go unanswered. In 1521 he was excommunicated and declared an outlaw by the church; but he was given personal protection by Frederick III, who may have felt sheepish about his own enormous collection of relics. Helped by the relatively new technology of printing, the views of Luther and his followers spread across Europe. At the heart of their "new opinion" lay the primacy of the Bible, the word of God, as opposed to the authority of the church through the pope or its councils.

In Germany itself the local princes, motivated more by power than theology, were divided into pro-Protestant and pro-Catholic factions whose mutual enmity was for a time resolved by the 1555 Peace of Augsburg—which laid down that a ruler's faith should determine that of his people. Elsewhere, Protestant ideas were developed more systematically: by Huldrych Zwingli in Zurich and, especially, by John Calvin in Geneva. In England, Henry VIII broke with Rome over the issue of divorcing his childless wife Catherine of Aragon. In 1534 Henry declared himself head of the Church of England and in 1536 set about suppressing monasteries and appropriating their lands for himself and his favorites. Henry himself showed no great enthusiasm for doctrinal change; but the ideas of the reformers gained ground during the reign of his successor, Edward VI, and—after the five-year reign of the Catholic queen Mary Tudor—during the time of Elizabeth I.

The reformers damaged pilgrimage both by attacking its underlying theological assumptions and by physically destroying shrines and relics. Luther, for example, in his *Address to the Christian Nobility of the German Nation* (1520), stated that going on pilgrimage deluded people into believing they were performing important virtuous acts. God, he said, had commanded us to look after our families and neighbors—not to go off to Rome on a spending spree, masking curiosity or "devilish delusion" with piety. Pilgrimages, he continued, were occasions for sinning, for flouting God's commandments, and for attracting ne'er-do-wells such as beggars and vagabonds. Secular and religious authorities should persuade would-be pilgrims to spend the money and time they were reserving for the journey on their families and the poor instead.

The reformers also attacked relics, purgatory, and prayers to the dead; and with their emphasis on justification by faith, and a person's direct relationship with God—unmediated by saintly intercessors—they challenged the traditional idea of the "communion of saints": the great family of Christians whose members, both on earth and in the afterlife, are locked in a reciprocal spiritual relationship. Removing the idea that a penitential journey to a shrine could help a relative in purgatory, or that a saint could intervene in human affairs, undercut the theological basis for pilgrimage. In the past, pious motives for going to Rome or Jerusalem may have cloaked worldly desires for a taste of freedom, travel, and new experiences—but the devotional aspect gave the journey an all-important focus, even if there were tempting distractions. Now, without a religious goal, there was nothing to stop pilgrimage from becoming a sightseeing trip, in which the novelties of travel would be an end in themselves.

In countries where the ideas of the reformers held sway, people did not suddenly reject the old piety en masse. But the pressure to change was powerful. In England the clergy were instructed to preach against pilgrimages to relics, and between 1536 and 1540 hundreds of monasteries and shrines were dissolved up and down the land. Bells were melted down, wooden choir stalls torn out, and lead stripped from the roofs. A contemporary chronicler remarked that "all the notable images unto the which were made any special pilgrimages and offerings, were utterly taken away."

Relics were declared to be fakes and broken up or burnt. To take a typical example, the bishop of Rochester in Kent declared the most sacred relic of Hayles Abbey—a vial said to contain the Holy Blood of Christ—to be nothing but "honey clarified and coloured with saffron" and destroyed it. And it was not only the relics that were stripped away: in Elizabethan times the Royal Injunctions of 1559 decreed that commissioners should "destroy all shrines, coverings of shrines [. . .] pictures, paintings, and all monuments of feigned miracles, pilgrimages, idolatry, and superstition, so that there remain no memory of the same in walls, glass windows, or elsewhere within their churches and houses." It was hard, nonetheless, to wipe out the memories. At Walsingham a government official alleged that a certain woman had dreamed up "a false tale" of a miracle effected by a statue of Our Lady after it had been carried off from the shrine and burned at Chelsea. Her punishment for declaring this story was to be confined to the stocks then paraded around the marketplace in a cart as a "reporter of false tales." The official added his view that "the said Image is not yet out of some of their heads."

But if the impulse to go on pilgrimage in search of miracles and cures is age-old and universal, what happened to this need in the Protestant lands? Without the healing power of saints to sustain them, many people would have turned to local herbalists, "wise women," and white witches for medicinal help. It may also be significant, as Ronald Finucane has observed, that spa resorts became more popular during Reformation times, with cured invalids leaving their crutches behind as they had formerly done at pilgrimage shrines.

Another, altogether different, approach to pilgrimage was suggested by Erasmus in "The Religious Pilgrimage." When Menedemus mentions doing the "Roman Stations," which traditionally meant visiting certain churches and altars in Rome, he goes on to explain exactly what his stations are: "I walk about my house; I go to my study, and take care of my daughter's chastity; thence I go into my shop, and see what my servants are doing; then into the kitchen, and see if anything be amiss there; and so from one place to another, to observe what my wife and what my children are doing, taking care that every one be at his business. These are my Roman Stations." In this view, pilgrimage is a way of life based around a domestic circuit of personal responsibility rather than a linear journey to an external destination.

Erasmus's idea of a bourgeois *peregrinus* signified a radical departure from the traditional notion of pilgrimage. Toward the end of the sixteenth century, a more secular approach to pilgrimage travel can be inferred from guidebooks such as the Protestant Jerome Turler's *De Peregrinatione*. This work addressed the practicalities of travel abroad in a way familiar from past pilgrim guides, but despite its title, it was concerned primarily with the importance of discovering and learning from strange but potentially useful foreign customs. This was pilgrimage as a fact-finding tour.

During this period there were also handbooks that conceived of spiritual journeying without any physical travel at all. The Spanish Dominican friar Luis de Granada (c. 1504–1588) saw pilgrimage as a spiritual act of imagination that had the advantage of avoiding the pitfalls of an actual journey with all its seductive curiosities. A similar idea of mental or imagined pilgrimage is also found in the *Spiritual Exercises* of St. Ignatius Loyola, published in 1548, which sets out a meditative journey that calls upon the reader to conjure up certain events and scenes from the Gospels and to use them as tools to help overcome his or her sense of sin. In a similar vein, the Strasbourg preacher Johann Geiler (d. 1510) declared that he had worked out exactly how long it would take to walk to Rome, go round the churches, and return home (forty-nine days in total, in his view), so that a prisoner unable to go there could reenact the journey in his mind by pacing round his cell for the right amount of time (seven weeks at seven miles per day). The French Jesuit Louis de Richeome published, in 1604, *Pelerin de Lorete*, an account of his pilgrimage to Loreto in Italy, but emphasizing how pilgrimage symbolized the human condition as well as the importance of prayer, meditation, and contemplation. In short, the point Richeome wanted to make was that a geographically located shrine was no substitute for arrival at the heavenly Jerusalem through the interior life.

The principle of being able to make a pilgrimage through the mind and heart also lay behind the traditional Catholic Stations of the Cross. These fourteen representations of the Passion of Christ are linked to events and locations in Jerusalem, from Jesus's condemnation by Pilate to his crucifixion and burial. Each image alludes to a scene from the passion and is used as a focus for specific devotions. From the fifteenth and sixteenth centuries onward it became increasingly common for images of the stations to be set up in churches all over Europe—these visual signs enabling the faithful who could not make the physical journey to Jerusalem to be "transported" there through an imagined empathetic journey.

During the first half of the seventeenth century, Europe was disfigured by widespread war, waged in the name of religion but mainly fueled by national politics. The Thirty Years' War (1618–48) pitted the Catholic Habsburg Holy Roman Empire and Spain against the Protestant German princes and their allies (including, at different times, Holland, Denmark, Sweden, England, and even Catholic France, anxious to curb Habsburg power). The war continued until the Peace of Westphalia in 1648 realigned territorial boundaries and confirmed the principle that a state's religion should be determined by its ruler.

In England, the religious tensions created among Anglicans, Puritans (Anglicans who wanted to see the Church of England further "purified" of Catholic elements of worship), Catholics, and Dissenters (non-Anglican Protestant groups such as the Independents, Presbyterians, and Baptists) were a constant problem to the Stuart kings. But the victory of Oliver Cromwell and the Parliamentarian forces during the English Civil War (sometimes called the "Puritan Revolution") and the establishment of the Commonwealth (1649–60) led to the ascendancy of the Puritans' interpretation of "true godliness." This included an emphasis on high personal moral standards, education, and plain dress.

The Puritans also stressed the primacy of the word of God, at the expense of ceremony. To them the idea of going on a physical pilgrimage, with its presupposition of relics and a cult of saints, was an alien one. Yet the fictional pilgrimage of one Puritan has become one of the most famous in the world. John Bunyan's *The Pilgrim's Progress*, first published in 1678 and expanded in 1684, is an allegorical pilgrimage of the soul related in such fresh, vivid, down-to-earth language that it quickly became universally popular, even among the barely literate. In the tradition of allegorical storytelling that went back to Guillaume de Deguileville's *Pilgrimage of the Life of Man* (c. 1330), Bunyan's story revolves around a pilgrim named Christian who leaves his home in the City of Destruction to journey to the Celestial City. Along the way he encounters various trials, tribulations, and temptations, but also encouragement from characters such as Piety and Charity. Eventually he crosses the River of Death and arrives at the Celestial City, which "shone like the sun, the streets also were paved with gold, and in them walked many men with crowns on their heads, palms in their hands, and golden harps to sing praises withal."

To create his masterpiece, Bunyan drew on his own conflict with the Royalist authorities of the Stuart Restoration—he was imprisoned for his faith off and on between 1660 and 1672—as well as his own crisis of faith and his knowledge of the Bible and popular preaching. Bunyan's pilgrimage is not a physical journey, nor does it resemble the concentrated meditations of Ignatius Loyola or the domestic prudence of Erasmus's "Roman Stations": it is a luminous journey of the soul, imagined but rooted in the word of God—a spiritual trek from the human condition of sin to the God-given state of grace.

———

Religious pilgrimage in post-Reformation Europe, then, especially in Protestant lands, fell out of fashion. As F. Thomas Noonan has noted, "The Levant became demagnetized as Europeans were drawn to new interests, new ambitions, new routes, new destinations." It was not only pilgrimage that suffered. In the eighteenth century, the so-called Age of Enlightenment, when the value of reason and empirical science seemed infectiously attractive to Europe's intelligentsia, devout spirituality and mysticism were often viewed with suspicion by the established churches (and dismissively labeled as "enthusiasm"). The Anglican bishop Joseph Butler once told John Wesley (1703–1791), the founder of Methodism, that "pretending to extraordinary revelations and gifts of the Holy Spirit is a horrid thing; a very horrid thing!"

The historian Edward Gibbon (1737–1794) is characteristic of the cool, ironic spirit of this age and its debunking of the spiritual ambience of ancient pilgrimage places. Summarizing the tradition of pilgrimage to Jerusalem, he wrote, "It might perhaps have been expected that the influence of the place and the belief of a perpetual miracle should have produced some salutary effects on the morals, as well as on the faith, of the people. Yet the most respectable of the ecclesiastical writers have been obliged to confess, not only that the streets of Jerusalem were filled with the incessant tumult of business and pleasure, but that every species of vice—adultery, theft, idolatry, poisoning, murder was familiar to the inhabitants of the holy city." The French diplomat and writer François-René de Chateaubriand, a devout Catholic who traveled to Jerusalem and the Holy Land in 1806, lamented that the "anti-religious" eighteenth century had undermined pilgrimage and its travel literature: "Nobody now reads the ancient pilgrimages to Jerusalem."

But the urge to go on journeys of inspiration—what might be an innate pilgrimage instinct—did not go away. Young well-off men and sometimes women, rejecting the traditional holy shrines of yore, set out to broaden their minds, widen their cultural knowledge, and improve their aesthetic taste in cities such as Paris, Geneva, Cologne, Florence, Rome, Venice, and Naples. Their "shrines" tended to be splendid works of architecture or art collections; their "pilgrim badges" were often antiquities, brought back home to adorn elegant drawing rooms and libraries.

The Grand Tour, as this cultural journey around Europe became known, had many similarities to pilgrimages: like medieval pilgrims, eighteenth- and nineteenth-century gentlemen were swindled by ferrymen, bitten by fleas, and fleeced by innkeepers, and they, too, had to traverse the treacherous Alps with guides, pay tolls, and bribe officials. They would also have shared the same excitement—or disappointment—at reaching their long-imagined goals. But whereas the pilgrim, at least notionally, was seeking the realm of the divine and the miraculous, the tourist primarily sought new experiences, education, and pleasure. Instead of kneeling at the shrine of St. Thomas Becket and donating a coin or two, he would stand and gaze at a Michelangelo sculpture and buy a guidebook.

The Grand Tour became particularly popular with young Englishmen after peace descended on Europe with the end of the Seven Years' War in 1763. Many, used to the restrained piety of the Church of England, found the unfamiliar sights and sounds of continental Catholicism exotic: the shrines with richly painted images of saints, the constant sound of bells, the religious processions, the high profile of monks and priests. But these manifestations of religion were more of a curiosity to the visitors from the British Isles than a stimulus to awe. An Irish traveler named Catherine Wilmot did find Milan Cathedral magnificent, but the local friar who talked to her of relics and miracles she dismissed as a "wholesale camel-swallower." James Boswell, Samuel Johnson's biographer, also admired the cathedral— but for its "many good pictures." Rome itself was often disappointing, with its beggars, narrow and dirty streets, and general air of poverty. Yet compensations were to be found in the noble ruins, squares, fountains, columns, and countless statues and paintings. The catacombs were visited, as were the main churches—Boswell even enjoyed a service at St. Peter's. The tourists studied their guidebooks, sketched, painted, scribbled down their impressions, and bought their souvenirs: these were their devotions.

The French Revolution and the Napoleonic Wars severely limited travel on the continent. There was a resurgence of activity after 1815, which Samuel Taylor Coleridge characterized in his poem "The Delinquent Travelers" as follows: "Tour, Journey, Voyage, Lounge, Ride, Walk, / Skim, Sketch, Excursion, Travel-talk— / For move you must! 'Tis now the rage, / The law and fashion of the Age." But from then on the Grand Tour never really recovered its former prestige.

Yet Italy always maintained its spiritual and artistic allure. Mark Twain wrote about it in *The Innocents Abroad* (1869), a book based on a trip with American companions to Europe and the Holy Land. His account shows how far the Western mind had changed since the days of the early and medieval church: "Day after day and night after night we have wandered among the crumbling wonders of Rome; day after day and night after night we have fed upon the dust and decay of five-and-twenty centuries—have brooded over them by day and dreamt of them by night till sometimes we seemed moldering away ourselves, and growing defaced and cornerless, and liable at any moment to fall a prey to some antiquary and be patched in the legs, and 'restored' with an unseemly nose, and labeled wrong and dated wrong, and set up in the Vatican for poets to drivel about and vandals to scribble their names on forever and forevermore."

In Britain, during these war-ravaged years on the continent, would-be travelers were forced to find substitutes: the mountains of Snowdonia for the Alps, or the Lake District for the Italian lakes. One celebrated homegrown site was Tintern Abbey, whose ruins beside the River Wye in Wales inspired paintings from J. M. W. Turner and a poem from William Wordsworth. The abbey's ivy-clad stone shell was perfect for the Romantic worldview—which delighted in nature in its wildest forms—though Revd. William Gilpin (1724–1804), author of a bestselling handbook on the Tintern area, thought the gable ends too regular: "[. . .] a mallet judiciously used (but who durst use it?) might be of service in fracturing some of them." With no relics, altars, statues, or chapels to lure the pilgrims to Tintern, visitors had to fall back on their imaginations to re-create a sense of the numinous, aided by the surrounding tree-clad hills and swiftly flowing river. Although there were no bells, candles, or incense to regale the senses, the spirits could be lifted by a Welsh harper hired at nearby Chepstow or by a midnight picnic, lit by flaming torches. Having no officially sanctioned religious pilgrimages to turn to, British Romantics of the late eighteenth and early nineteenth centuries had to invent their own.

16

ORTHODOX PILGRIMAGE

*"The Holy City [Jerusalem] is placed amidst ravines
and hills, and the sight thereof is wondrous . . ."*

John Phocas, a medieval Byzantine pilgrim

Pilgrimage has always played an important part in the Eastern
Orthodox tradition, and to this day crowds of pilgrims can
be seen at many shrines throughout the Orthodox world. As with
Catholicism, the foremost pilgrimage shrine for Orthodoxy is Jerusalem and the Church of the Holy Sepulchre. Eastern Christians have
also paid reverence to countless other shrines and sanctuaries, such
as St. Catherine's in the Sinai Peninsula, Rila in Bulgaria, or Trinity–
St. Sergius in the city of Sergiyev Posad (near Moscow), where people
come to venerate the relics of St. Sergius. The Orthodox spiritual and
pilgrimage tradition is also distinguished, as we shall see, by the value
placed on icons, or sacred images, as well as the idea of the "wandering pilgrim."

The Eastern Orthodox Church is one of the largest branches of
Christianity and consists of a number of self-governing churches
that are in religious communion with each other. They include the
churches of Greece and Russia—historically the two most important

ones—but also the churches of Bulgaria, Romania, Serbia, and others. Orthodox Christians share an ancient heritage with Roman Catholics, but Orthodoxy does not recognize the universal authority of the pope, and there are also different emphases on the liturgy and variations in doctrine.

The Orthodox Church emerged in the centuries after Emperor Constantine I made Christianity the most favored religion in the Roman Empire in the early fourth century and developed the city of Constantinople (today's Istanbul). From then on the empire had two capitals, Rome in the west and Constantinople in the east, and Christianity developed in these centers in different ways. After the eclipse of the Western Roman empire in the fifth century, the Eastern empire gradually became known as the Byzantine Empire. Over the centuries, political and theological friction between the Eastern, Byzantine, Greek-speaking church and the Western, Roman, Latin-speaking church eventually led to a formal schism between them in 1054. The relationship between the two churches then plummeted after the sack of Constantinople in 1204 by a force of western European crusaders, who, after killing their fellow Christians and plundering the city, installed one of their leaders as the new Latin ruler of the Byzantine Empire. The regime lasted for nearly sixty years.

Orthodoxy remained centered on Constantinople until the Ottoman Turks captured the city in 1453, after which it lost its spiritual authority: church buildings became dilapidated, the training of priests deteriorated, and clerical appointments were subject to corruption. But as the Orthodox Church declined in Greece and Asia Minor, it began to flourish elsewhere, particularly in Russia, and especially after Ivan III had destroyed the power of the Tatars in Muscovy in 1480. Just over a hundred years later a patriarchate was created in Moscow, and in the following centuries the Russian Church forged a close relationship with the national government—up until the 1917 revolution.

As mentioned above, the Holy Land has always been the most sacred place for Orthodox pilgrims. The Byzantine pilgrim John Phocas traveled to the Holy Land in the late twelfth century and visited a number of well-established sacred sites, including Cana, Nazareth, and Jerusalem itself, where he marveled at the Church of the Holy Sepulchre. After Jerusalem he made his way to a number of small desert monasteries, as well as Bethlehem and Mount Carmel.

Another Eastern pilgrim was a monk named Daniel of Kiev, who set out in the early 1100s from his monastery and made his way overland to Palestine (at this time largely under Crusader control) by way of Constantinople. He lived in and around the Jerusalem area for more than a year, visiting the holy places. Although he reports that "Every Christian is filled with an immense joy at the sight of the holy city of Jerusalem; and tears are shed by the faithful," Daniel's record of his pilgrimage is more descriptive than emotional, and he lists, without elaboration, a great number of what had become standardized pilgrim sites, such as the Mount of Olives, the Church of the Holy Sepulchre, and the tomb of St. Stephen.

In his account, Daniel makes it clear that he is writing about the holy places for the benefit of those who might not ever travel to Palestine. He also points out that the benefits obtained by doing charitable works are in themselves an equivalent to the blessedness of arriving at a pilgrimage shrine, a sentiment that foreshadowed the trend in late medieval Western piety in which the inner journey gained as much emphasis as—or even more than—the outer one. As Daniel writes, "Many virtuous people, by practicing good works and charity to the poor, reach the holy places, without leaving their homes [. . .] Others, of whom I am the chief, after having visited the holy city of Jerusalem and the holy places, pride themselves as if they have done something meritorious, and thus lose the fruit of their labor."

Alongside holy places that it has shared with Western Christians, such as the sites of the Holy Land, Eastern Orthodoxy has always had its own special pilgrimage destinations, for example the churches of Byzantine Constantinople, the island of Patmos, and the monasteries of Mount Athos. One of the most venerable sanctuaries is the Orthodox monastery of St. Catherine's on the Sinai Peninsula. Built in the sixth century, St. Catherine's is associated with St. Catherine of Alexandria, a fourth-century martyr who, by tradition, was tortured on a spiked wheel by the Roman emperor Maxentius and then beheaded. Her relics were then miraculously transported to the site of the monastery by angels. Pilgrims made the journey to this isolated part of the world to see various holy sites in and around the monastery.

Another historic Orthodox monastery that has attracted pilgrims down the centuries can be found on the Greek island of Patmos, near the coast of Turkey. Patmos is famous as the place where John allegedly received the vision that was written down as the book of Revelation in the New Testament. For centuries pilgrims have walked up from the island's harbor of Skala on a winding track that leads to the town of Chora and the fortress-like monastery of St. John, built in 1088 on the ruins of a Greek temple dedicated to the goddess Artemis.

Back on the Greek mainland, in the north of the country, Mount Athos has drawn spiritual seekers from medieval times. The complex comprises twenty Orthodox monasteries that nestle on the easternmost of the three prongs of Greece's Halkidiki peninsula. Set on steep, forested hillsides overlooking the Aegean, the first monastery was established in the tenth century. From this time on, other monastic communities were founded, including those belonging to the Serbian, Bulgarian, and Russian churches. As well as a timeless atmosphere of meditation, there are priceless sacred treasures to be found on Athos, such as icons, relics, manuscripts, chalices, and the like. But pilgrimage there is not straightforward. Female pilgrims are not allowed to visit (because of a perceived threat to the monks' celibate and contemplative way of life) and male pilgrims have to obtain a special permit. Nevertheless, Athos draws a constant, if relatively small, number of male pilgrims from all Christian denominations. Its austere atmosphere, remoteness, refined spirituality, and otherworldliness make it stand out among pilgrimage destinations.

———

St. Catherine's Monastery, Patmos, and Mount Athos survived the Ottoman conquests in the eastern Aegean and Middle East; but many shrines and holy places that were pilgrimage centers for Eastern Christians became difficult or impossible to access during this time, including the churches and monasteries of Constantinople and especially the church of Hagia Sophia. It had inspired pilgrims with its huge dome, vast interior space, lofty columns, silver iconostasis, and glittering icons and mosaics since the sixth century. But after the Ottoman conquest of Constantinople, Hagia Sophia was converted into a mosque, and today welcomes visitors as a museum.

Before its fall, Constantinople attracted a steady stream of Orthodox pilgrims. One of these was a certain Stephen of Novgorod, who arrived there around the middle of the fourteenth century and was awestruck by the size and splendor of the city and of Hagia Sophia. He described how he and his companions walked around the church "with tears of rejoicing," marveling at the number of oil lamps on the walls and in recesses and the aisles, lighting up great icons. There were "beautiful purple stone columns" as shiny as mirrors, a fountain of holy water, and marble columns "with relics of the saints reposing within them" against which people would press parts of their bodies that needed healing. Stephen and his friends encountered Isidore, the patriarch of Constantinople, in the church and "kissed his hand, for he is very fond of Rus."

One of the motives of Orthodox Christians for making a pilgrimage was, and still is, to gain divine help from visiting and venerating an icon. For Western Christians it has usually (but not always) been a relic of a saint, enclosed in a sumptuous reliquary, that has provided the sacred center of a pilgrimage destination. Orthodox Christians place great value on relics, too, but they especially have a long tradition of venerating icons, which they regard not simply as sacred works of art designed to heighten the viewer's emotions, but as revelations of God through line and color, windows directly into the spiritual world. This means that icons are highly stylized and created according to a strict tradition regarding what the figures look like, and the artist is not free to experiment as he desires.

Icons were such a central feature of the Byzantine world that it is perhaps not surprising they were at the center of the violent iconoclast ("icon-breaking") controversy that lasted more than a century. In 726 the Byzantine emperor Leo III, citing the second commandment ("You shall not make for yourself a carved image, or any likeness of anything that is in heaven above, or that is in the earth beneath, or that is in the water under the earth"), demanded that all icons be destroyed. A bitter struggle ensued between iconoclasts and the pro-icon faction, the iconodules. The iconoclasts initially gained the upper hand, but the iconodules eventually won the war, and in 842 Empress Theodora officially restored the veneration of icons.

Orthodox Christians also venerate the relics of saints. At the monastery of Rila in Bulgaria, for example, pilgrims have been visiting the relics of the hermit saint John (d. 946) for hundreds of years. Other relics that continue to draw pilgrims are those of the Russian saint Sergius of Radonezh (1314–1392) and the Greek saint Luke (tenth century), whose bones reside in the monastery of Hosios Loukas.

The story goes that Luke went to live as a hermit near the town of Distomo in central Greece, among the ruins of an ancient Greek temple. A few years after his death, a church was built to house his remains, and the monastery complex of Hosios Loukas evolved from the church. An architectural gem of the Byzantine period, Hosios Loukas is built of stone and terracotta and consists of two churches, a bell tower, a crypt, monks' cells, and courtyards. Pilgrims came to smell the healing fragrance that Luke's tomb was said to emit and also to sleep next to it in order to receive an incubatory dream of a cure.

As is the case in Western Europe, there has always been a tradition of the inner as well as the outer journey in the Orthodox world. This emphasis is perhaps best exemplified by the age-old Orthodox practice of hesychasm, a form of mystical prayer that is often performed in combination with breathing techniques. The specific form of prayer most associated with hesychast practice is known as the Jesus prayer, which consists of saying repeatedly the words "Jesus Christ, Son of God, have mercy on me."

The Jesus prayer became popular in Russia through teachers such as Seraphim of Sarov (1759–1833), and especially after the publication in the later nineteenth century of an anonymous spiritual text called *The Way of a Pilgrim*, which connected prayer and the idea of pilgrimage as a quest. *The Way* tells the story of an unnamed wandering pilgrim traveling around the country (in a manner not dissimilar to an Irish *peregrinus*) trying to find someone who will enlighten him about St. Paul's words "pray without ceasing." Eventually he discovers a mentor in a monk who teaches him how to say the Jesus prayer and instructs him to repeat it first three thousand, then six thousand, and finally twelve thousand times a day. This induces a deep contentment in the pilgrim.

He continues his journey, living off scraps, sleeping rough, and having memorable encounters with peasants, criminals, monks, and priests. He also receives guidance from his now-deceased mentor in dreams. Gradually he learns how to concentrate on his heart while reciting the prayer, and this brings about euphoric spiritual states: "My heart would feel as though it were bubbling with joy, such lightness, freedom, and consolation were in it." *The Way of a Pilgrim*, which has become a classic text in Russian and Orthodox spirituality, indicates a particular emphasis on pilgrimage: a journey not so much to one specific shrine but a wandering, a seeking, a pilgrimage that aims to deepen the soul and pave the way to enlightenment or unity with God.

17

MODERN SHRINES

"Who can estimate the holiness and perfection of her, who was chosen to be the Mother of Christ?"

John Henry Newman, *Parochial and Plain Sermons*

The great age of medieval pilgrimage ended with the Reformation. But while many pilgrim shrines in Protestant countries were dismantled, there were exceptions: St. Winefride's Well at Holywell in Wales, for example, has attracted pilgrims from medieval times to the present without interruption. And there were probably various unrecorded local shrines in Protestant lands that continued to draw small numbers of pilgrims.

In Catholic countries, pilgrimage was still a meritorious act. But the Catholic world, too, had to face the cold winds of skepticism, reason, and secularization that eroded pilgrimages. Of the great medieval shrines, Santiago de Compostela retained its pilgrimage tradition the best and even experienced a revival in the late seventeenth century before declining in the eighteenth, with the onset of the turmoil caused by the French Revolution and the Napoleonic Wars. And the Santiago pilgrimage revived once more in the late twentieth century.

Another place that bucked the downward trend of pilgrimage in the early modern world was Czestochowa, Poland's greatest shrine. Today Czestochowa is an industrial city, but its spiritual center remains the monastery of Jasna Góra ("Shining Mountain," named for the hill it is built upon), which houses the famous icon of the Virgin Mary known as the Black Madonna. This image may be a copy of an ancient Byzantine icon. It arrived at Jasna Góra in the Middle Ages and became nationally revered after 1655, when the monastery withstood a siege by a powerful Swedish army. The Polish king John Casimir then dedicated the country to the Virgin Mary, recognizing the monastery and the icon as its sacred center. Since then the shrine has survived another attack by the Swedes, in 1702, the partition of the country in the eighteenth century, World War II, and Communist rule.

The growing emphasis on reason and scientific principles in Europe in the seventeenth and eighteenth centuries was naturally inimical to pilgrimage. But during the course of the nineteenth and early twentieth centuries, pilgrimage reawakened: new pilgrimages came into being and old ones were resuscitated. The reasons for this development are difficult to establish. Increasing industrialization and mechanization of society may have resulted in a longing for rituals that gave a sense of *communitas*. At a time when science, and in particular the theory of evolution, was challenging the authority of the Bible and old certainties of faith, pilgrimage may have partially answered a need for direct religious experience—a thirst for connecting with places and people seemingly in close contact with the divine.

Another, more mundane, spur to renewed pilgrimage was transport: steamboats and trains could now cover in days journeys that would have taken weeks to accomplish by sail or on horseback. The nineteenth century saw the start of "package" vacations, pioneered by Thomas Cook, a British entrepreneur with a Baptist background. In 1876, *Cook's Tourists' Handbook for Palestine and Syria* provided essential information for travelers, but did not assume they were devout pilgrims. In a section on the Church of the Holy Sepulchre it notes, "Whatever may be the emotions of the traveler, as he enters this most remarkable place in the world, he should at least tarry awhile to observe, respectfully, the feelings of others; and no one can witness the passionate devotion of pilgrims without emotion."

One of the characteristics of some of the new pilgrimage destinations was that they did not revolve around the holy relics or images typical of medieval times, but reputed miraculous apparitions, especially of the Virgin Mary. The church authorities generally took, as they still do, a conservative approach to them, carefully weighing up the evidence before making a definitive statement about their authenticity.

France in the 1800s proved to be fertile ground for these apparitions. (Sociologists of religion are tempted to connect them with the fact that the country was recovering from one of the most turbulent periods of its history, with first the Revolution and then the Napoleonic Wars.) Between July 1830 and September 1831 a French religious novice named Catherine Labouré saw, in her convent chapel in Paris, four apparitions of the Virgin Mary, who commanded her to have a medal struck bearing the Virgin's image: in the following years millions of "Miraculous Medals" were duly made. In 1846 two children at La Salette near Grenoble claimed to have seen a vision of the Virgin, who appeared as a radiant form wearing a gold-sequined robe and silver shoes. In 1858 a girl named Bernadette Soubirous reported seeing the Virgin near the town of Lourdes. Thirteen years later, in 1871, two boys said they had seen the Virgin in an apparition in their hamlet of Pontmain in northwestern France, during the time of the Franco-Prussian War.

But it was not just in France that apparitions of the Virgin occurred. In 1879 she was apparently seen by villagers in Knock in Ireland, and in 1917 by three peasant children at Fátima in Portugal. Between November 1932 and January 1933 in the small town of Beauraing in Belgium, five children allegedly saw apparitions of the Virgin thirty-three times. From 1961 to 1965, it was the turn of Spain, when four girls in the village of Garabandal claimed to see numerous apparitions, mostly of the Virgin Mary. And in 1981, six young people in the village of Medjugorje in Bosnia allegedly received apparitions of the Virgin Mary.

———

Apparitions of the Virgin Mary to one or more individuals, resulting in the creation of a shrine (and a pilgrimage connected to it), had, of course, happened many times prior to the nineteenth century—including the vision of Pope Liberius that was reputedly instrumental in the building of the church of St. Mary the Greater (Santa Maria Maggiore) in Rome, and the vision received by a Mexican peasant named Juan Diego in 1531, resulting in the construction of a shrine dedicated to Our Lady of Guadalupe. In medieval England, the shrine of Walsingham was founded after a devout noblewoman, Lady Richeldis, spoke of visions of the Virgin Mary.

Although there have been many precedents for apparitions of the Virgin Mary over the centuries, the question remains, why these alleged visions in the modern era? And why the Virgin Mary? The veneration of the mother of Jesus goes back to ancient times, and depictions of her were made in the catacombs of Rome. For Christians she has always been the "Theotokos," Mother of God (she was proclaimed as such by the Council of Ephesus in 431), who is the mediatrix between people and God and therefore a figure of veneration. By the fifth and sixth centuries, churches in Rome were being dedicated to her, such as Santa Maria Antiqua, Santa Maria Maggiore, and Santa Maria in Trastevere. In the Middle Ages, devotion to Mary deepened, prayers and hymns to her became more popular, cathedrals were dedicated to her (for example at Chartres in France and Salisbury in England), and countless Marian artworks created.

After the Reformation, Protestant countries rejected or downgraded Marian devotion. But the mother of Jesus has always remained a central figure in Catholic worship. In 1854 Pope Pius IX formally declared the dogma of the Immaculate Conception, which states that Mary was preserved from the "stain of original sin" at the instance of her conception.

A number of these modern apparitions have occurred at times and in places when war, oppression, poverty, and the like have been the cause of widespread suffering. The fact that the shrines then built have subsequently prospered from pilgrimage "tourism" has obviously raised the eyebrows of skeptics. On the other hand, it may be that in hard times people pray, consciously or subconsciously, with far more devotion and intensity than they would do otherwise. Those who believe in the power of prayer would not find it hard to countenance the idea that at such times the channels of communication, greatly intensified, might result in a visual manifestation of a divine figure. And, since Mary has always had a role as a mediatrix, it is not so surprising that manifestations of the divine should frequently be of her.

Whatever their causes, the Marian apparitions in the nineteenth and early twentieth centuries began a new phase of pilgrimage in the modern world, with the creation of what have become some of Christianity's most popular shrines.

On February 11, 1858, a poor, illiterate fourteen-year-old girl named Bernadette Soubirous claimed to have seen an apparition of the Virgin in a grotto near her hometown of Lourdes at the foot of the Pyrenees. This and subsequent apparitions transformed an obscure French town into one of the most frequented places of Christian pilgrimage in the world, with millions of pilgrims visiting each year.

The apparition was the first of eighteen that Bernadette was to receive over the following five months. At first, it was not certain who or what the young woman of the apparition was. Bernadette simply referred to her as *Aqueró*, the local dialect word for "that one." The reactions of local people were mixed. One of the nuns who taught Bernadette accused her of playing pranks. Others believed she had seen the ghost of a devout Lourdes woman named Elisa Latapie, who had died the previous autumn. After the sixth apparition the civic authorities began to get involved, the local police commissioner trying in vain to pressure Bernadette into admitting her story was a hoax. After the ninth apparition, when Bernadette was seen to scrabble around in the mud inside the grotto and uncover a spring of water, she was interrogated by a local magistrate, who made her promise not to return to the spot. But the pull of the cave proved irresistible.

The parish priest, Father Peyramale, was also unsympathetic at first. But he was forced to confront the issue head-on when, after the thirteenth apparition, Bernadette informed him that *Aqueró* had instructed her to tell "the priests" that people were to come to the grotto in procession and that a chapel must be built. Peyramale retorted testily that he would have to know the apparition's identity before there was any question of processions or a chapel. During the sixteenth apparition, on March 25, the feast of the Annunciation, Bernadette duly asked the young woman who she was. She replied in the local dialect, *"Que soy era Immaculada Councepciou"*—"I am the Immaculate Conception."

It seemed incredible to Peyramale that an uneducated peasant girl could have made up such a phrase, and from then on he became one of Bernadette's staunchest supporters. There were still two apparitions to come. On April 7, in the presence of about a thousand onlookers, Bernadette appeared to let the flame of the candle she was holding lick her hand without showing signs of pain—an event that afterward many hailed as a miracle. The final apparition occurred on July 16, 1858, after the grotto had been cordoned off by the authorities to keep the crowds away, and Bernadette was forced to catch her final glimpse of *Aqueró* from the far side of the river.

For Bernadette the apparitions were the climax of her time on earth. There were no more visions, voices, or beatific states. The remaining years of her short life were relatively uneventful and colored by her constant struggle against illness, a sad irony since Lourdes would become known as a great healing shrine. In 1860 she left her poverty-stricken family to live in the local hospice run by the Sisters of Charity. Six years later she was admitted to the Sisters' mother house at Nevers in central France. There she resided for the rest of her life, removed from the world, consoled by the memory of that radiant young woman she had once seen. She died in 1879, at the age of thirty-five.

While Bernadette gradually faded into relative obscurity after the apparitions (though she was eventually made a saint in 1933), Lourdes and its grotto grew steadily more famous. One reason for this was a series of seemingly miraculous healings at the shrine. Other important factors were encouragement from the imperial French household of Napoléon III and his wife, Empress Eugénie, as well as the energetic support of the dynamic Catholic thinker and journalist Louis Veuillot.

But although popular enthusiasm for Lourdes began to grow, the church treated the affair with caution—not wishing to invite charges of credulity from its critics—and investigated Bernadette's apparitions through a commission, which, after four years of deliberating, declared them genuine in 1862. The church also began to build the chapel *Aqueró* had requested on land it had bought above the grotto. In 1866 the Crypt of the sanctuary was completed, and in the same year the railway came to Lourdes, greatly increasing the influx of pilgrims from all over France.

One major motive for making the pilgrimage was, and still is, the hope of a cure for sickness. The first recognized healings at Lourdes occurred as early as March 1858, during the time of Bernadette's apparitions. Again, the church trod carefully with these and other alleged cures and set up a commission to investigate them. Later on, in 1883, the Medical Bureau was founded to bring more rigor and impartiality to the process of recognizing cures (and the Medical Bureau was supplemented by another medical committee in 1947). It is a measure of the church's caution that of the many thousands of reported cures, to date fewer than seventy have been formally recognized as miracles.

Lourdes continued to grow in prestige throughout the closing decades of the nineteenth century. In 1873, two years after France's humiliating defeat in the Franco-Prussian War, a national annual pilgrimage to Lourdes in the month of August was inaugurated by the Assumptionists, a religious order who saw the pilgrimage as a way of reasserting Christian values against a tide of secularism and, as Ruth Harris has noted, "to encapsulate and channel a mood of national soul searching." The numbers of pilgrims increased year by year, with more than 30,000 arriving by train in August 1897, having endured cramped, stifling carriages, with the sick and dying laid out on stretchers, attended by doctors, nurses, nuns, friends, and relations.

After their arrival at Lourdes pilgrims were confronted, as they still are, with a town of two distinct parts: the main residential and commercial area—and the Domain of Our Lady, comprising the land around the grotto. The most visible building in the Domain is the Basilica of the Immaculate Conception (commonly known as the Upper Basilica), constructed above the grotto and consecrated in 1876. In front of the Upper Basilica and the Crypt is a third sanctuary, the Basilica of Our Lady of the Rosary, consecrated in 1901. Framing the complex are two long, curving ramps that rise from the ground on arches to the level of the Upper Basilica. Nearby is the Basilica of St. Pius X, a huge underground structure, consecrated in 1958, which can hold about 20,000 people.

As for the grotto, it is still the town's spiritual epicenter. An esplanade was built beside it, allowing the pilgrim crowds to gather there to pray, light candles, or proceed to the nearby baths to immerse themselves in freezing water piped from the grotto's spring.

What is curious about Lourdes is not so much that it became a Marian shrine but that it should become the preeminent one in Europe. Certainly its setting has helped. The cliffs, river, woods, and mountains combine to create a mystique that rises above the rampant commercialism of the town. Bernadette's story also carries a compelling mythic power, especially in the way that events slowly gathered momentum, drawing in more and more people until even "hardened officials" could not resist their force. It is also interesting that Bernadette was not the only person to see apparitions at Lourdes: a number of local children claimed similar visions soon after her experiences. Most of these were dismissed as false, but a few had an air of authenticity, especially those experienced by a girl named Marie Courrech, who was highly regarded for her innocence and strong faith. Yet only Bernadette was officially accredited as the unique recipient of apparitions of the Virgin.

Another curious aspect of the Lourdes story is the nature of *Aqueró*, whom Bernadette described as a girl of about her own age dressed in simple clothes, rather than the maternal figure of most other Marian apparitions. Indeed, Bernadette did not at first identify her as Mary; and in an area in which belief in folklore was deeply rooted it must have seemed significant to some that she referred to the apparition as a *damizéla*, a word often used to mean a fairy. The turning point came when *Aqueró* declared unequivocally that she was the Immaculate Conception. For the church, these words could mean none other than the Virgin Mary.

Yet even with the church's approval of the apparitions, Lourdes's success cannot be fully explained: pilgrimage sites cannot thrive on official patronage alone. The answer may lie in the fact that Lourdes has maintained its reputation as a place of physical, spiritual, and emotional healing over many decades. It is a place that gives hope to those for whom all other remedies have failed. It may be that some physical conditions apparently cured at Lourdes have had psychosomatic rather than "organic" causes, as skeptics tend to believe (though this does not invalidate the idea of a miraculous cure); or that some cures have more to do with mental determination than supernatural agency; or that witnessing the sick and dying bearing their travails patiently, and the selflessness of their helpers, not only lifts the spirit but has a positive physical effect. In short, the causes for cures effected at Lourdes, partial or permanent, must ultimately remain a mystery; but many have no hesitation in calling that mystery God.

In 1879, twenty-one years after the events at Lourdes, a group of about fifteen people saw another seemingly miraculous appearance of the Virgin Mary, at the village of Knock in County Mayo in the west of Ireland. Like Lourdes, Knock was a poor, obscure place, suffering from the political, social, and economic hardships of the times. The harvest of 1879 had failed, and widespread famine had ruined livelihoods and rendered tenants unable to pay landlords. Evictions were rife. Many emigrated to America or England. Others took heart from the newly formed Land League, which used mass rallies and intimidation to fight back against rack-renting landlords.

Unlike at Lourdes, however, the Knock apparition happened on only one occasion (lasting for about two hours) and imparted no verbal message. Yet it was enough to turn Knock into one of the world's great modern Marian shrines. This did not happen overnight. For the first twenty-five years after the event, Knock drew a steady stream of pilgrims. But in the first quarter of the twentieth century numbers dwindled until, in 1929, the local archbishop of Tuam unofficially endorsed the shrine by going on pilgrimage there. From then on Knock flourished. Over the next fifty years it gained increasing recognition from Rome, which culminated in 1979—the centenary year of the apparition—with the visit of Pope John Paul II.

Knock grew physically, too, and the village of humble cottages became a town lined with guesthouses, hotels, restaurants, and souvenir shops. The original church of St. John the Baptist, where the apparition had taken place, was remodeled. Next door to it the huge new Basilica of Our Lady was dedicated in 1976; a large hostel, folk museum, and the more intimate Chapel of Reconciliation were added to the site later. In 1985 the first flights from the new Knock airport set the seal on the shrine's global status.

Knock has few aesthetic pretensions. But the shrine area is well designed and functional; and from May to October, the crowds filing in to attend mass, the hum of pilgrims reciting their rosaries, and the innumerable candlelit processions create a powerful sense of the numinous.

The extraordinary two hours that created the Knock phenomenon occurred on the rainy evening of August 21, 1879. The parish priest's housekeeper, Mary McLoughlin, was on her way to visit a neighbor named Mrs. Byrne when she allegedly saw what looked like statues standing in front of the south end of the church. Thinking the priest had acquired them from Dublin for some purpose, she thought nothing more of it. Half an hour later, Mary McLoughlin left Mrs. Byrne's house in the company of the latter's daughter, Mary Byrne. The two women passed the church and both again saw the "statues." Suddenly Mary Byrne exclaimed that they were moving and identified one of the figures as the Virgin Mary.

Mary Byrne ran off to tell others and soon a small group of villagers—ranging from six to seventy-six in age—had gathered to contemplate the scene. What they saw through the pouring rain were three human figures, all standing about two feet off the ground. In the center was the Virgin Mary, wearing a crown and white cloak, her hands raised, as if in prayer. To her right was St. Joseph, slightly bowed in deference to the Virgin. To her left was a figure whom they took to be St. John the Evangelist. He had his right hand raised, as if he was preaching, held an open book in his left hand, and wore a bishop's miter. To St. John's left was an altar with a lamb standing on it in front of a cross.

The tableau was bathed in glowing light, which one witness saw from half a mile away. The figures were three-dimensional, but they did not speak and when people approached them, they receded toward the south wall. One woman, Bridget Trench, tried to kiss the feet of the Virgin, but found them insubstantial; she also discovered that the ground beneath the figures was dry. None of the witnesses fell into a rapture, but all were filled with profound awe.

After half an hour Mary McLoughlin went off to tell the priest, Archdeacon Cavanagh, about the apparition; but he failed to be impressed enough by her story to go out and see it—a great irony since afterward many locals believed they had been granted the apparition precisely because of the priest's holiness. (He later fully believed in the apparition and was the first effective supporter of the shrine.) After a while, a couple of others also departed because it was raining so hard. Then finally a woman named Judith Campbell went off to check up on her sick mother and, finding that she had collapsed, rushed back to the church to tell the others. They immediately ran over to help the woman (who died a couple of weeks later), and when they returned to the church they found the figures had gone.

News of the apparition spread through the village, then the county and the whole country. In October a church commission examined fifteen of the witnesses and pronounced their joint testimony as "trustworthy." Skeptics down the years have pointed to the fact that the apparition succeeded in bringing much-needed money into the locality—that is, there could have been a strong economic motive for the miracle. And there were suggestions at the time that phosphorescent paint or a magic lantern might have been used to create the effect, though these were soon discounted since they failed to address the point that allegedly the figures were three-dimensional, that the ground underneath was dry although it was raining, and that the light could be seen half a mile away. Nor did the event bear the hallmarks of mass hysteria and hallucination: the witnesses were calm and lucid, and Mary McLoughlin and Mary Byrne at first interpreted the figures rationally as statues. Could it have been a prearranged conspiracy? Or, put another way, how would it be possible to show it had not been a conspiracy? The testimony has seemed consistently truthful to believers and skeptics alike, and the church gave no credence to several other apparitions reported at Knock in 1880.

In any case, unofficial groups of pilgrims began arriving at Knock within weeks. Many began to chip off pieces of cement from the south wall in the hope they would effect a cure—some dissolved them in water which they then drank. In 1882 the archbishop of Toronto, who was visiting, noted a vast number of crutches and sticks lining the south wall—left behind by those who had apparently been cured—and an "iron railing around the ends of the church to prevent the pilgrims from again removing the plaster from the gable." Today the south wall is enclosed by a glass-fronted chapel, through which a tableau of white marble statues can be seen, representing the figures of the apparition.

One of the unusual aspects of the Knock apparition was the lack of a verbal message, and speculation as to its meaning has perforce focused on the visual symbolism. The lamb on the altar recalls the description in John's Gospel of Jesus as "the Lamb of God, who takes away the sins of the world," as well as the image of the Lamb standing on the throne in the Book of Revelation. As such, it perhaps represents the sacrifice of Jesus and his ultimate triumph over death. Of the three human figures, Mary and Joseph conformed to traditional representations. The bishop-like figure was construed to be St. John the Evangelist by Mary Byrne, because she had seen a statue of the saint in a similar pose at the church of Lecanvey near Westport on the coast of Mayo.

But it may also be that theological interpretation misses the point. Certainly what struck the Knock witnesses most was the apparition's miraculous nature and its beauty—so strange and intense that it made some, including the twenty-year-old Dominick Byrne, burst into tears and left Bridget Trench with the feeling that the "figures and the brightness would continue there always." The youngest of the witnesses, six-year-old John Curry, told the church authorities that he saw "the fine images and the light, and heard the people talk of them, and went upon the wall to see the nice things and the lights." Almost six decades later, in 1936, Curry was again questioned by the church about the apparition—and he said that he would remember the figures "till I go to my grave."

————

As with Lourdes and Knock, the genesis of the village of Fátima in Portugal as one of the great modern pilgrim shrines was due to an apparition, or series of apparitions, of the Virgin Mary.

Fátima lies about eighty miles north of Lisbon, and in 1917, like the rest of Portugal, the village was suffering from the hardships incurred by World War I. As Portuguese troops joined the battlefront farming declined, food became scarcer, and prices soared. In addition, the church was being oppressed by the Republican government, which had come to power in 1910 and was enacting anticlerical policies, suspecting the church of being in league with the ousted monarchist party.

Fátima follows the pattern of Lourdes and Knock as a place suffering from social, political, and religious problems; and like the other two shrines, it has benefited materially from the many thousands of pilgrims who made, and make, their way there every year. The correlation between the miraculous and economic hardship might seem suspicious to some observers, but believers could argue that it is precisely among the needy that faith is at its strongest. This, however, still does not explain what marked out Fátima (or Lourdes or Knock) as the location of a Marian apparition, since there must have been countless other equally downtrodden places in the country.

It was three peasant children—Lucia dos Santos and her two cousins, Francisco and Jacinta Marto—who reported the visions. They lived in a small village neighboring Fátima, which in 1917 was only a hamlet. They used to graze their sheep in fields in and around a natural depression called the Cova da Iria, about a mile from Fátima. It was in this setting at about noon on May 13, 1917, a bright cloudless day, that they saw a flash of lightning and then, above a small scrubby tree, a ball of light enclosing a Lady "dispensing light, clearer and more intense than a crystal cup full of crystalline water penetrated by the most glaring sun." According to the children, the Lady told them she was from heaven but did not disclose her name at first, instead instructing them to come back to the same spot every month for the next five months, after which she would reveal her identity. She also told the children that they would suffer because of humanity's sin, and she finished by opening her hands and letting two beams of light unfold, filling them with a sense of divine radiance. Allegedly the Lady also relayed a message in three parts to the children: The first two parts revealed a terrifying vision of hell and seemed to indicate that although World War I would come to an end, another great conflagration would happen in the future. The third part of the message, disclosed by the Vatican in May of 2000, consisted of a disturbing and apocalyptic vision in which a bishoplike figure, wracked with sorrow, was passing through a ruined city, praying along the way for the souls of dead people he came across, before being shot dead by anonymous soldiers.

The children kept their rendezvous with the Lady on June 13, when they were accompanied by a small crowd of curious onlookers. Again the Lady allegedly appeared above the tree to the children (she was invisible to everyone else) and told them they must recite the rosary. She also said she would take Jacinta and Francisco to heaven very soon but that Lucia would remain on earth. By July 13 nearly three thousand people had gathered to watch as the children saw the Lady return, bathing them, as they felt, in radiant light and revealing her message to them. Matters went awry on August 13, when the children were snatched away to the town of Ourém by the hostile local Republican administrator, who tried to force them to reveal the Lady's message. Despite threats of being boiled alive in oil, the children said nothing and were released. Although they missed their meeting with the Lady, she did appear six days later and said she would perform a miracle at her last appearance "so that all shall believe."

By September 13 the crowd was bigger than ever and included a number of high-ranking priests, who had come to observe what by now was a well-publicized phenomenon. As at Lourdes and Knock the church was cautious, wishing neither to alienate the thousands who believed in the children, nor to appear superstitious and gullible and thereby play into the hands of its enemies. This time some of the crowd claimed to see a "globe of light" slowly move toward them, but not the Lady herself, whom only the children saw; they said the Lady told them to keep saying the rosary and reassured them that next month she would perform a public miracle.

On October 13 there were an estimated seventy thousand people gathered in the rain at the Cova. The midday deadline came and went. Then out of the gray skies, as the children reported, the Lady appeared to them in a flood of white light and announced to them that she was the Lady of the Rosary and that a chapel must be built in her honor. The children also saw St. Joseph, the Child Jesus, and other representations of the Lady—grieving as Our Lady of Sorrows, then crowned as the Queen of Heaven. Then the crowd allegedly witnessed the promised miracle: the sun appeared as a bright silver disk and began to "dance"—spinning like a Catherine wheel, flinging out streams of flame, and bathing the earth in the colors of the rainbow. Then it seemed to vibrate and plummet, zigzagging toward the onlookers. People fell to their knees in swaths, crying aloud in terror or bursting into tears, thinking the world was coming to an end. Just as suddenly, the orb began to withdraw to the sky and resumed its ordinary place as the sun.

The "miracle" has remained a mystery. Skeptics and atheists saw it, hostile Republican newspapers described it, and individuals who were not expecting anything spotted it from up to thirty miles away. Some of the crowd, it must be said, did not see it. But thousands did. There was no suggestion of the event being an eclipse or any other measurable astronomical phenomenon, and it still remains baffling to those who wish to interpret it rationally. For believers, there were few precedents for what happened. It is highly unlikely that anyone there knew that a nineteenth-century Scottish folklorist named Alexander Carmichael had recorded the vision of a woman named Barbara Macphie, seen from a hill in Scotland at Easter: "the glorious gold-bright sun [. . .] rising on the crests of the great hills, and it was changing colour—green, purple, red, blood-red, white, intense white, and gold-white, like the glory of God of the elements to the children of men. It was dancing up and down in exultation at the joyous resurrection of the beloved Saviour of victory." Unlike Macphie's joyful vision, however, the Fátima sun seems to have provoked mainly fears of catastrophe and doom.

Founded on the extraordinary apparitions and boosted, in 1930, by the endorsement of the church, Fátima grew as a place of pilgrimage and became established as one of the foremost shrines in the world, especially after World War II, when hotels, hostels, and other facilities were built for the annual surge of pilgrims between May and October. The most visible sanctuaries at Fátima are the Basilica of the Most Holy Trinity (completed in 2007), which is a sleek, low, circular structure that can hold about nine thousand worshippers; and the Basilica of Our Lady of the Rosary of Fátima, begun in 1928 and consecrated in 1953. The latter's 200-foot spire rises high above the colonnaded plaza that stretches out in front of it, where vast crowds gather on holy days. The heart of Fátima, however, is the Chapel of the Apparitions, where a pillar topped by a statue of the Virgin Mary commemorates the spot where the Lady is believed to have appeared to the three children.

Whereas Lourdes is strongly associated with healing, and Knock's apparition offered a glimpse of divine beauty, the key note at Fátima was penance, the consciousness of sin, and the need for reparation in order to avert a global disaster. This warning from the Lady, coupled with the apocalyptic sign of the "dancing sun," seems to suit the mentality of the nuclear age. At Lourdes the magnetic center is the small, intimate earthly grotto; at Knock it is the original church; and at Fátima it is difficult not to keep glancing up at the sun.

18

SANCTUARIES
IN THE AMERICAS

*"And behold an angel of the Lord appeared in front
of her [St. Anne] and said: 'Anna, Anna, the Lord
has heard your prayer, and you shall conceive and
bear a child that shall be spoken of everywhere in
the world.'"*

The Infancy Gospel of James

Alongside the great historical pilgrimages in Europe such as
Rome, Santiago de Compostela, and Canterbury, and, in modern times, Lourdes, Knock, and Fátima, a vibrant pilgrimage tradition exists in the Americas.

The most famous Christian shrine in the Americas is arguably the Basilica of Our Lady of Guadalupe in Mexico City. The focus of the Guadalupe pilgrims is an image of the Virgin Mary, which is believed to have been miraculously imprinted on a cloak. It is housed in the basilica. The legend says that in December 1531, an indigenous peasant (and convert to Christianity) named Juan Diego received an apparition of a woman on Tepeyac Hill, in what is now a neighborhood of Mexico City. He had been drawn there by unearthly singing and the sound of his name being called by a female voice. Talking to Juan Diego in his native language, the woman revealed herself to be the Virgin Mary and told him he had to go to the bishop and ask him to construct a chapel on the hill where she had appeared.

According to the legend, Juan Diego did as he was commanded, but the bishop dismissed him out of hand. Juan returned to Tepeyac Hill, and the Virgin told him to try the bishop again the next day. This time the bishop demanded to see a "sign" that Mary had really spoken to him. Juan Diego reported this to Mary, and she told him to return to her the following day. Although delayed by seeing his very sick uncle, he did manage to meet the Virgin again, and she reassured him about his uncle's condition. She also directed him to a spot on the hill where he found some beautiful roses—an extraordinary discovery given that the flowers were not the sort to grow there, and especially not in the month of December. He gathered some of the roses in his cloak, or *tilma*, and brought them to the bishop. The latter was amazed to see not only the flowers, but, even more so, an image of the Virgin imprinted on the cloak.

In due course a shrine was built at Tepeyac in the Virgin's honor, and replaced in 1709 by a larger church, now called the Old Basilica. In the 1970s a new basilica, capable of holding ten thousand people, was built.

The revelations of Juan Diego and the events that followed were later considered to be a stepping-stone in the relationship between Christianity and native faiths in Mexico. Some commentators have argued that there had been a culture of oppressors (the Spanish conquistadors) imposing an alien faith (Christianity) upon the oppressed (the Aztecs and other native peoples)—but that when Juan Diego was granted visions of the Virgin Mary, there was a sea change. Other commentators believe that the process of integration between the new and old religions took much longer and that the Virgin of Guadalupe had much less immediate impact. They argue that the Catholic Church took its time to assess and confirm the status of the shrine and the cloak, pointing out that a feast day—December 12—was officially granted only in 1754.

In any case, the ripple that began with Juan Diego's visions continued to flow outward from the epicenter of Tepeyac down the years, gathering strength in the twentieth century. In 1910 Pope Pius X declared that the Virgin of Guadalupe was the patroness of Latin America. In 1990 Pope John Paul II beatified Juan Diego, and nine years later he declared that Our Lady of Guadalupe was the patroness of the Americas. On July 31, 2002, the pope canonized Juan Diego.

The December pilgrimage to Our Lady of Guadalupe has now become an extraordinary mass spiritual and national event. Pilgrims come from all over Mexico during the week before the 12th, and music, dancing, and parades set the tone for the festivities. Many put on historic native costumes, including headdresses that spray out rainbow-colored feathers, and carry replica images of the *tilma* or statuettes of the Virgin Mary. Some walk the last part of the journey across the basilica plaza on their knees.

The circular new basilica itself, its roof sweeping up and gathered in the center like a tent, is deceptively cavernous. Inside, the *tilma* is displayed high on the wall behind the altar.

The shrine of Our Lady of Guadalupe started with Juan Diego's vision on the hill of Tepeyac. It has now become one of the most influential Catholic sanctuaries in the Americas and spawned other shrines, such as the Cathedral Santuario de Guadalupe in Dallas, Texas; the Santuario de Nuestra Señora de Guadalupe in Monterrey, Mexico; and the Shrine of Our Lady of Guadalupe in La Crosse, Wisconsin. From being a local patroness, the Virgin of Guadalupe has become an international symbol of healing and protection, a figure special to the religious and national consciousness of Mexicans, but also one that represents the amalgamation of different faith traditions.

————

Located some twenty miles northeast of Quebec City, the shrine of Sainte-Anne-de-Beaupré—dedicated to St. Anne, the mother of Mary and grandmother of Jesus—holds a central place in the lives of many French Canadians and is widely known for its healing powers. From its foundation in 1658, the sanctuary has maintained a reputation for being a place where seemingly miraculous cures occur, as crutches, canes, and other ex-voto offerings preserved within the basilica bear witness.

The sanctuary and the local cult of St. Anne date from the early days of France's colonial ambitions in Canada. The city of Quebec, in what was then New France, was founded in 1608 and began to prosper from its trade with France and the French West Indies, as well as by being the administrative headquarters of the new colony. According to tradition, sometime in the 1650s French sailors were imperiled by a storm on the St. Lawrence River and vowed to honor St. Anne if they would escape a watery grave. They survived and decided to build a wooden chapel at what was then called Petit-Cap, near where the basilica now stands.

Why did these sailors pray to St. Anne? Anne is in fact a somewhat mysterious figure; she is not mentioned in the New Testament, and legends about her appeared only in apocryphal Christian writings. It is said she was married to a man named Joachim and that they remained childless for many years. Eventually each received a vision of an angel, who informed them that Anne would bear a child and that they must greet each other with the happy news at the Golden Gate in Jerusalem. The couple's meeting at the gate later became a popular subject for painters, including Giotto, Lippi, and Dürer. Anne duly gave birth to Mary.

Her status as the mother of Mary and grandmother of Jesus solidified during the early centuries of the church. The Byzantine emperor Justinian I dedicated a chapel to Anne in Constantinople in the sixth century, and it is believed that Pope Constantine (r. 708–715) brought her cult to Rome, from where it spread westward. Many churches were dedicated to Anne, including, in France, Sainte-Anne d'Auray, near Vannes; Sainte-Anne-la-Palud on the Finistère coast; and Sainte-Anne de Robien in the town of Saint-Brieuc.

In Quebec, the building of the promised chapel began in 1658, and it was during the start of the construction that the first miracle associated with the chapel occurred. Allegedly, a local man named Louis Guimont, suffering from an acute affliction, placed three stones in the chapel's foundation and was healed. News of Guimont's cure spread and the first pilgrims began to arrive. In 1665 Marie de l'Incarnation, founder of the Ursuline order in Quebec, reported that in the nearby "church dedicated to St. Anne [. . .] Our Lord is working great marvels [. . .] the paralytics walk, the blind can see, and the sick are healed of every kind of illness."

The sanctuary has been rebuilt down the centuries. A stone church built in 1676 lasted until 1876, the year St. Anne was proclaimed patron saint of Quebec. It was replaced by a basilica more commensurate with St. Anne's growing prestige and the rise in the number of pilgrims. Finally, after a fire in 1922, a new basilica rose from the ashes of the old, which is the one pilgrims now visit. It was built of local granite in the neo-Romanesque style. Its harmonious facade comprises a main portal set beneath a large rose window and flanked by two 300-foot-high towers.

It might be more accurate to describe Sainte-Anne-de-Beaupré as a sacred complex, with various chapels, gardens, and a museum, than simply as a solitary basilica. Inside the church itself there are two levels, the main floor and a chapel on the lower floor, and there is a broad array of sacred art—paintings, mosaics, sculptures, and many stained-glass windows—as well as some holy relics of St. Anne herself.

The focus for pilgrims is the painted oak statue of St. Anne by the basilica's north transept: crowned and richly robed, she stands in glory on top of a pillar and is framed by symbolic spikes of golden light; she bears in her arms the infant Mary. Behind the statue, the Chapel of St. Anne holds a relic donated by Pope John XXIII in 1960, namely a piece of Anne's forearm that is kept inside a gold reliquary shaped like a forearm.

Countless pilgrims come to the shrine every year, to pray to St. Anne and, perhaps, to ask for a cure for themselves or for others. For many visitors, St. Anne, the "Good Grandmother," offers the prospect of solace and healing.

———

The town of Chimayo lies about twenty-five miles north of Santa Fe in New Mexico. Remote though it may be, Chimayo welcomes every year many thousands of pilgrims, who come to visit its small, compact nineteenth-century church, El Santuario de Chimayo. Their purpose is to worship God, to venerate a wooden crucifix known as Our Lord of Esquipulas—and to touch, or stir into water and drink, or even eat, earth that is believed to have curative properties and which can be accessed from an exposed part of the church's floor. The collection of crutches, photographs, and votive candles left behind by grateful visitors cured of their ailments by their pilgrimage explains why Chimayo has been dubbed the "Lourdes of America."

Like other pilgrimage shrines, Chimayo has its own foundation legends, and stories about how the crucifix was found. It is said that in around 1810, a local man named Don Bernardo Abeyta was carrying out ritual penances on Good Friday night when he saw a brilliant light rising from a site in Chimayo. He investigated the source of the light and discovered it was emerging from the ground. He began digging, and to his amazement uncovered a large wooden crucifix.

On three occasions a priest from nearby Santa Cruz tried to install the crucifix in his church. But each time it mysteriously returned to the place of its discovery—so it was decided to build a chapel to house it there. This chapel was duly built and lasted for a few years until, in 1816, the church that stands today was completed. (It remained in the possession of Abeyta's descendants until 1929, when ownership was transferred to the Catholic archdiocese of Santa Fe.)

The shrine sits at the heart of a small compound, with a walled-in courtyard in front of it that pilgrims enter through an arched gate. The facade of the adobe church is dominated by two small towers. Inside the church, wooden wall panels of colorful folk art depict saintly Christian figures. At the end of the nave, beyond the altar, stands the crucifix of Our Lord of Esquipulas.

For many visitors, however, the sacred center of the church is a small room adjoining the nave which houses *el pocito*, the "little well." This is a small hole, cut into the floor, which contains holy earth. Pilgrims scoop the earth into receptacles to take home, or rub it on their bodies there and then.

While Chimayo may lack the great stained-glass windows and soaring pillars of cathedrals and basilicas, it offers visitors a deeply spiritual way to step out of the modern secular world.

———

One of the largest churches in the world, the Basilica of Our Lady of Aparecida, in the town of Aparecida in southeast Brazil (about midway between Rio de Janeiro and São Paulo), is the most visited Christian shrine in South America. Millions of visitors make their way there each year to venerate a small clay statue of the Virgin Mary, a Black Madonna alleged to have miraculous powers. On October 12, Our Lady of Aparecida's feast day and a national holiday, tens of thousands of worshippers visit the basilica to celebrate mass.

According to legend, the statue of the Virgin was found in a local river in the year 1717. Three devout fishermen were casting their nets in the river but struggling to catch the fish they needed to feed a visiting high-ranking official. Their luck changed when one of their nets brought up the headless statue of a female figure, shown with her hands raised to her chest in prayer. Then their net also caught the statue's head. The three men realized they had found a representation of the Virgin Mary, and right away they began to catch plenty of fish. They took the statue back to their village, where its head and body were reattached. Before long it was credited with healing and other divine powers—a belief aided by the story of its "miraculous" appearance in the river (hence the name "Aparecida," which means "appeared" in Portuguese).

The worship of Our Lady of Aparecida grew, and in 1745 a chapel was built to house the statue. A century later, to accommodate the increasing number of visitors, work on a larger sanctuary began; it was completed in 1888. (Today it is known as the Old Basilica.) In 1930 Pope Pius XI declared Our Lady of Aparecida to be Brazil's patron saint. Over the years the need for an even larger church became apparent, and in 1955 construction began on a new, vast basilica, which was consecrated by Pope John Paul II in 1980. It can hold up to 45,000 worshippers.

Enshrined in a niche in the basilica, the statue of Our Lady of Aparecida is adorned with a gold crown and draped in a dark blue, richly embroidered cape. Across Brazil, models of the statue are displayed in homes and businesses, miniatures of it are worn around the neck, and depictions are ubiquitous, from stickers to postcards. When Pope Francis visited Aparecida in July 2013, he said in his homily at the shrine, "Whoever would have thought that the site of a fruitless fishing expedition would become the place where all Brazilians can feel that they are children of one Mother?"

Since the start of the new millennium a pilgrimage trail to Aparecida for hikers and cyclists has been set up. Known as the Caminho da Fé, the Way of Faith, it runs for about three hundred miles through southeastern Brazil. The Caminho da Fé is still in its infancy, but with its contrasting landscapes—including sugarcane and coffee plantations, mountains, woods—and variety of footpaths, dirt tracks, and paved roads, it offers visual delights and physical challenges aplenty.

On arrival in Aparecida, pilgrims are greeted by the full paraphernalia of a major pilgrimage site, including an expansive parking lot and numerous shops selling sacred souvenirs. But any sense of commercialization is put into perspective by the small clay statue of the Virgin in the basilica's interior.

19

REVIVING THE PAST

"For holy angels, the citizens of the heavenly country, clad in white robes and flying with wonderful speed, began to stand around the saint while he prayed."

Adomnan of Iona, *Life* of St. Columba

Apart from the rise of new pilgrimage shrines such as Lourdes, Knock, and Fátima, the late nineteenth and early twentieth centuries also witnessed the revival of a number of medieval places of pilgrimage, such as Iona, Canterbury, Glastonbury, and Walsingham in Britain, and Croagh Patrick in Ireland (which had seen some decades of reduced activity in the later 1800s). These revived shrines drew upon their centuries-old spiritual inheritance (if not a return to the original cult of saints and relics) to attract new generations of pilgrims. Nowadays they also attract those concerned with contemporary spiritual issues such as social welfare, ecology, and the unity of the church. What they have lost in medieval intensity and ritual, they have gained in greater openness and informality.

Ireland's holiest mountain and reputedly a place of Christian pilgrimage for more than fifteen hundred years, Croagh Patrick ("Croagh" comes from the Irish *cruach*, meaning "mound") rises from the southern edge of Clew Bay near the town of Westport, about thirty miles west of Knock. Its unique shape and setting by the sea make it an object of beauty as well as reverence, as the English writer William Makepeace Thackeray observed in his *Irish Sketch Book* (1843): "[. . .] it is clothed in the most magnificent violet-colour, and a couple of round clouds were exploding as it were from the summit, that part of them toward the sea lighted up with the most delicate gold and rose colour."

Known locally as the Reek (from the word "rick," as in a "stack"), what makes this majestic cone-shaped mountain sacred is the legend that in the year 441 CE, St. Patrick spent the forty days and nights of Lent fasting on top of its peak. According to the medieval *Book of Armagh* and the *Tripartite Life of St. Patrick*, the saint was assailed during his vigil on the Reek by multitudes of demonic black birds—so many that "he knew not heaven or earth." His attempt to drive them off with "maledictive psalms" failed, so he resorted to striking his bell—so vigorously that it could be heard across the country—before flinging it at his assailants: "No demon came to Ireland after that till the end of seven years and seven months and seven days and seven nights." After his successful efforts to dispel the black birds, Patrick sank to the ground weeping with relief and was rewarded with the sight of a consolatory angel and a flock of melodiously singing white birds—which have been traditionally identified as the choirs of Ireland's saints past, present, and future, gathering around Patrick to join him in blessing the people of Ireland.

By tradition Patrick also drove the poisonous snakes and other reptiles of Ireland from the mountain into the sea. That Ireland was famed for being free of reptiles was certainly well known to the Venerable Bede, who wrote that "there are no reptiles, and no snake can exist there" and that its very air would kill any such creatures on a ship approaching the country. Bede also reported that a common remedy for snakebites in England was to drink water in which "scrapings" from Irish books had been steeped.

There are scattered references to the Croagh Patrick pilgrimage in chronicles and other records down the centuries. In 1113, for example, the *Annals of Ulster* state that lightning killed thirty people fasting on top of the mountain on St. Patrick's Day, March 17. In 1432, Pope Eugene IV granted an indulgence to pilgrims climbing the mountain, while in 1652 a priest by the name of James O'Mahony referred to the Reek pilgrimage as the most widely celebrated in the country. In the 1790s a Frenchman, the Chevalier de Latocnaye, visited (but did not climb) the mountain and mentioned in his account of his travels the bell with which Patrick had fought off the black birds: "[In the local chapel] is a black bell for which the inhabitants have a peculiar veneration. It is used as a thing to swear on in legal matters, and no one will dare to perjure himself on it."

At some point the bell (which is thought to date from between 600 and 900 CE) was removed from the chapel and kept by members of the local Geraghty family, from whom it was purchased by Sir William Wilde (Oscar Wilde's father) in about 1840. Wilde wrote that the bell was taken to the top of the mountain on Reek Sunday (the last Sunday in July, when the annual pilgrimage takes place) and placed in the chapel, where pilgrims were allowed to kiss it for a penny. If a pilgrim suffered from rheumatism he could pass it three times around his body for two pence. Eventually the bell, which is known as the *Clog Dubh* ("Black Bell"), ended up in the National Museum of Ireland in Dublin.

Shortly after Wilde bought the bell, Thackeray gave a good description of the pilgrimage crowds when he arrived at the Reek in his horse-drawn car: "The whole mountain was enveloped in mist; and we could nowhere see thirty yards before us. The women walked forward, with their gowns over their heads; the men sauntered on in the rain, with the utmost indifference to it. The car presently came to a cottage, the court in front of which was black with two hundred horses, and where as many drivers were jangling and bawling; and here we were told to descend."

A couple of years later, the catastrophic famine struck Ireland (from 1845 to 1848), decimating the population through death and emigration. In the decades that followed, the Croagh Patrick pilgrimage declined in popularity. But in the early 1900s, the archbishop of Tuam, John Healy, and a local priest named Michael McDonald set about breathing fresh life into the ancient pilgrimage. One major step was to build a new oratory on top of the mountain. There had been a chapel of some sort on the peak for as long as anyone could remember, reputedly going back to the times of Patrick (indeed, excavations in the 1990s revealed signs of settlement on and around the mountain reaching back several centuries before the Christian era). But what had survived of the chapel into the early twentieth century was no longer adequate for the saying of mass or for prayer. McDonald hired a local architect and building contractor, who erected the new sanctuary with a workforce of twelve men, laboriously carrying bags of sand, cement, and girders up the mountain by donkey, horse, and hand. On July 30, 1905, the oratory was dedicated by Archbishop Healy at a gathering of some ten thousand people.

Today many thousand pilgrims, some barefoot, make the annual ascent on Reek Sunday. Although the mountain is not particularly high (about 2,500 feet), the going can be rough over stretches of shale. The ascent begins with a long but relatively gentle climb past a welcoming statue of St. Patrick to a level ridge where, the habitual mist permitting, the plains and hills of Connemara suddenly sweep into view to the south. To the north the myriad islets of Clew Bay (one, it is said, for every day of the year) break up the rippling lines of the sea. On the ridge, devout pilgrims walk seven times around a mound of stones—the first of three stations—reciting Our Fathers, Hail Marys, and the Creed. From this ridge there is a final vertiginous and arduous ascent to the very top, a small plateau where pilgrims can sit down and gaze out toward the Atlantic Ocean—or, as part of the second station, walk around the chapel and "St. Patrick's Bed," the traditional spot where the saint slept during his period of fasting. The final station, three mounds of stones, lies to the west of the summit.

Climbing Croagh Patrick takes a matter of hours, usually from three to five. But for many pilgrims the strain, discomfort, frequent recourse to willpower, if not prayer, and ultimate elation during that short but intense time encapsulate the highs and lows of longer pilgrimages. Unlike at Knock, where the journey might have become secondary to the shrine and the practice of ritual devotion, the Croagh Patrick pilgrimage is as much about traveling as it is about arriving. It is a pilgrimage in which the natural elements—the mist and unexpected vistas of sea and distant hills, the sudden changes from clear blue skies to monotonous gray rain, the spontaneous words of encouragement passed like batons of friendship between pilgrims—all contribute to a sense of the pilgrim experience of *communitas*, a feeling of participating together in an exhilarating spiritual enterprise.

———

The tiny island of Iona off the west coast of Scotland has been a place of informal pilgrimage since the time when the Irish saint Columba (or Columcille, meaning "Colum of the church") founded a monastery there in the year 563. During the early medieval period, Iona became known for its dedicated monks and missionaries, who journeyed to mainland Britain to convert pagans, strengthen the faith, and establish other monasteries, notably Lindisfarne in northeastern England. After his death in 597, Columba was buried on Iona and his body remained there until the Viking raids of the ninth century, when his bones were carried to safety in Ireland. So although St. Columba is inextricably linked with Iona, the island did not develop the sort of tomb- or shrine-based cult that occurred in Santiago de Compostela or Canterbury, for example. In a way, the saint's shrine is Iona itself, with its natural jewels of emerald fields, golden beaches, and amethyst heather.

What has undoubtedly helped to revive the popularity of Columba and his island as a pilgrimage center in the twentieth and early twenty-first centuries is the association with modern "Celtic Christianity." This somewhat blanket term refers to an approach to the Christian faith that involves informal ways of worship and emphasizes the natural world and human creativity—celebrating the divine through music, dance, painting, and writing. Columba fits this idea well: he himself was not only a mystic and a lover of nature but also a poet and an assiduous copyist of manuscripts (one story claims he was sent into exile as a punishment for copying a manuscript without permission). According to the medieval Old Irish *Life* of the saint, his writing fingers were "as candles which shone like five bright lamps"; and there are a number of ancient Irish poems attributed to Columba. Although many of these date from later times, they do suggest he had a reputation for writing about God and nature—a world of birdsong and wild winds and seas.

Over time the island itself has gained a reputation for inspiring artists as well as other free spirits. Iona may not have grandiose monuments for the heart and mind to respond to—there is only a small restored medieval abbey and a scattering of hallowed ruins—but this very lack of a central shrine frees the imagination, allowing it to rove over the landscape and its many connections with Columban legends. In short, what Iona has is spiritual atmosphere. This barely expressible sense of being on a different spiritual plane moved even the habitually down-to-earth Samuel Johnson, who visited the island in 1773, to declare, "That man is little to be envied, whose patriotism would not gain force upon the plain of Marathon, or whose piety would not grow warmer among the ruins of Iona." The island inspired both John Keats and William Wordsworth to write about it after visits there in 1818 and 1835, respectively; and Felix Mendelssohn, in a letter from Glasgow dated August 1829, wrote that in "some future time I shall sit in a madly crowded assembly with music and dancing round me [. . .] I shall think of Iona with its ruins of a once magnificent cathedral, the remains of a convent, the graves of ancient Scottish kings."

Mendelssohn and Sir Walter Scott (whose Highland tour in the summer of 1810 included Iona) both found melancholy among the beauties of the island, with Scott remarking on the wretchedness of the inhabitants. In fact the island had been in steady decline since 1561, when the medieval Benedictine abbey built on the site of Columba's original monastery was dismantled by order of the Reformation authorities. The buildings gradually disintegrated and the island passed into lay hands, at first to the Macleans and then, in 1693, the Campbells. The revival of Iona's fortunes began only in 1874, when restoration was started on the abbey church. Then, in 1899, the chief of the Campbells, the eighth duke of Argyll, returned the abbey to the care of religious authorities by donating it to the Church of Scotland.

Nearly forty years later, in 1938, a visionary minister of the Church of Scotland, George MacLeod, founded the Iona Community—an event that has arguably done more than anything else to put post-Reformation Iona back on the spiritual map. Brought up in a wealthy family in Glasgow, MacLeod joined the Church of Scotland after serving in World War I, a traumatic experience that made him determined to help the victims of society. Working in a severely underprivileged area of Glasgow, MacLeod set about trying to help the poor, the unemployed, and others whom he felt society had failed. It was to implement his ideas on social justice and action that he founded the Iona Community. With the help of thousands of volunteers he restored the island's abbey and made it the heart of an ecumenical Christian community, as well as a center for retreats and programs of spiritual renewal. The community now has about 250 members who live throughout the world and are committed to a rule that involves "a daily devotional discipline, sharing and accounting for their use of time and money, regular meeting, and action for justice and peace." Since the death of MacLeod in 1991, the Iona Community has continued to emphasize issues such as social justice, economic action to alleviate poverty, and ecological concerns.

This stance on worldly matters may seem a far cry from the mystical, nature-loving figure of Columba depicted by his medieval biographers. But the community's religious perspective does in fact reflect the dynamic, practical side of the saint—a side that is often overlooked. Though deeply spiritual, Columba was also a hard-nosed, energetic man of the world, as unsqueamish about getting involved in local politics as he was ardent in his vigils and devotions to God.

Columba was born in Donegal, in the northwest of Ireland, in 521. With a family tree that included Niall of the Nine Hostages, high king of Ireland in the late fourth century, Columba grew up into a confident, able, and determined man of God. He founded a number of monasteries in Ireland, including Derry, Durrow, and Kells. The turning point of his life came in 563 when he set sail from Ireland, "desiring to seek a foreign country for the sake of Christ," as his seventh-century biographer Adomnan recorded—indicating that Columba was behaving in the manner of a typical Irish *peregrinus*.

Columba sailed from Ireland with twelve companions and settled on Iona—the first landfall, so the story goes, from which he could look back and not see his beloved country. They set about creating their monastery, building huts out of wood and wattle, erecting a church, sowing crops, and hunting seals for food and lamp oil. Once established, the Irish brethren were ready to move eastward and begin their mission to convert the pagans on the Scottish mainland—the indigenous Picts as well as settlers from Ireland (who, confusingly, were known as "Scots").

Little is known about the Picts. They were probably descendants of Scotland's Iron Age tribes, and their name ("painted ones") suggests they painted or tattooed their bodies. Their society seems to have been hierarchical, with a king at the top and soldiers, priests, craftsmen, and peasants below him. They may have encountered Christianity before Columba's arrival, through earlier missionaries and trading contacts with England and Ireland; but it was the endeavors of Columba that posterity remembers, honoring him as the father of Scottish Christianity.

Much has to be inferred about Columba's missionary work from the few details that remain; he must be imagined making frequent sorties from Iona, impressing Pictish chiefs with his unshakable faith and personal confidence, challenging pagan priests to trials of spiritual strength, organizing converts, and acting as a counselor and diplomat to local rulers. After bouts of fervent activity he would retreat to Iona and devote himself to the monastic life, praying, contemplating, copying manuscripts, welcoming guests, and guiding his brethren and organizing the practicalities of their existence.

Pilgrims to Iona today find plenty of historical and mystical associations from the past, but they also discover a living spiritual tradition in the work of the Iona Community. Its members maintain the abbey, conduct religious services, and lead spiritual retreats, themed workshops, and guided tours and walks; they also provide modest accommodation for a few dozen visitors at any one time. According to Adomnan, Iona was the scene of many miracles; and, as pilgrims have remarked down the ages, it is a place that makes you feel something out of the ordinary could happen. The eighth duke of Argyll referred to the island's "atmosphere of miracle," and George MacLeod said that the division between the material and the spiritual on Iona was only "paper-thin." It is this indefinable quality that draws pilgrims to Iona to this day.

———

In the Middle Ages, Walsingham, near the north coast of Norfolk, was second only to Canterbury as England's greatest pilgrim destination. It was the home of the shrine known as the "Holy House," said to have been modeled on the house of the Virgin Mary at Nazareth. As mentioned, the chapel was "full of marvels" and included a glass vial of breast milk reputedly from the Virgin Mary. Walsingham eventually came to grief in 1538 during the Reformation, and the towering priory to which the shrine was attached became a ruin (only one elegant arch now remains). As visitors ceased to come, what was once a thriving pilgrimage center dwindled to a place with a fading past and no future. According to an anonymous Elizabethan ballad, "Owls do scrike where the sweetest hymns lately were sung, / Toads and serpents hold their dens where the palmers did throng. / Weep, weep, O Walsingham, whose days are nights, / Blessings turned to blasphemies, holy deeds to despites."

In the late nineteenth century, however, the blasphemies began to turn back to blessings. Walsingham's revival began in 1894, when a devout Anglican named Charlotte Boyd bought and restored the dilapidated medieval Slipper Chapel, which stands about a mile from the main shrine. (Its name may have come from pilgrims taking off their shoes there before walking the last part of the pilgrimage barefoot.) Charlotte Boyd then converted to the Catholic faith and presented the chapel to the Benedictine Order, and it has become the Catholic National Shrine of Our Lady. In 1897 the first Catholic pilgrimage to Walsingham in some 350 years took place, from the Norfolk town of King's Lynn to the Slipper Chapel.

The Protestants joined in this spirit of revival in the 1920s when the local Anglican vicar, Alfred Hope Patten, installed in the parish church of St. Mary a new statue of Our Lady of Walsingham (modeled on an image of her on the priory's medieval seal), thereby providing a focus for Anglican pilgrimage. In the 1930s a new Anglican shrine complex was built near the ruins of the old priory, featuring a shrine church in which a replica of the Holy House was placed. The new statue of Our Lady was duly moved to the shrine church from the parish church and placed in a niche above the altar, gently illuminated by candles. In the following years both Catholics and Anglicans continued to respond to the revival, and once again "sweet hymns" were sung in Walsingham as pilgrims processed through its streets.

According to its foundation legend, Walsingham first became a shrine in 1061, five years before the Norman conquest of England. In that year, a local well-to-do widow named Richeldis de Faverches received a vision of the Virgin Mary, who revealed to her the house in Nazareth where the Annunciation had taken place and where the Holy Family had lived after the birth of Jesus. The vision of the Holy House was repeated two more times, and Mary instructed Richeldis to memorize its dimensions and to build a replica on her estate.

Richeldis was not sure where to place the shrine, until one morning she woke to see what she interpreted as a divine sign: on one of her fields were two rectangular dry patches in the heavy dew. Having to choose between the two spots, she told her workmen to raise the wooden structure on the one nearest to two wells. But as hard as they tried, the men were somehow unable to begin their building work. Disgruntled after a day of frustration, they left their tools and materials on the ground and went off home. That night Richeldis prayed for guidance, and as she did so the Virgin Mary and her angels erected the house on the other patch—much to the astonishment of the workers when they discovered it the next morning.

The Walsingham story echoes the pattern and motifs of other Christian foundation legends, for example that of St. Mary the Greater in Rome and its miraculous snowfall; or the Holy House of Loreto, near Ancona in Italy, which was said to have been transported by angels from Nazareth to Italy in 1295. There is also the story of the early medieval Welsh saint Brannock, who struggled to build a church in the north of Devon at what is now the village of Braunton, until he received a vision in which an angel told him to build where he saw a sow suckling her piglets. Shortly afterward, Brannock saw the sow on a meadow near a stream and duly built his church there. Such legends emphasize the grace-given origins of the shrines, and that human ingenuity and craftsmanship can never be of the same order as divine creation.

Walsingham's Holy House gradually became famous throughout the land. In the twelfth century a priory was constructed on the site, incorporating the wooden shrine within its walls. At a time when European armies were going off to Palestine on Crusade, the priory with its Holy House served for many people as a substitute pilgrimage destination, a small corner of the Holy Land tucked away in rural East Anglia: Walsingham became known as England's Nazareth. Down the centuries, to the time of Henry VIII and its dissolution, the shrine was well patronized by kings, queens, and nobles, becoming prosperous from various gifts of land, money, and jewels. Pilgrims came from all over the country and from abroad; those arriving from the south traveled by way of Newmarket, Swaffham, and Fakenham, while those from the north tended to gather at King's Lynn before walking east to Walsingham.

Along these routes, hostels and wayside chapels catered for the pilgrim groups, which included, according to a fifteenth-century ballad, the blind, the lame, the deaf, and lepers, as well as, wrote William Langland, "false hermits" who "went to Walsingham with their wenches after." The climax of the journey was a visit to the priory and the chapel that contained the Holy House, which, when Erasmus visited it, was a small wooden building with a door on each side to allow for the constant flow of pilgrims. It was dark, sweet-smelling, and lit only by tapers that made the offerings of gold, silver, and gemstones glitter. It also had an altar and a statue of the Virgin—undistinguished, Erasmus thought, in size, material, and craftsmanship, but "most efficacious in virtue." Another stop for pilgrims, especially the infirm, was the priory's two wells and sunken bath, where they could bathe or drink the holy water—which was recommended for headaches and heartburn—or fill their flasks with it to take back home. After the Reformation, the wells became "wishing" wells—a secular transformation that was often the fate of holy wells, such as St. Margaret's Well at Binsey in Oxfordshire.

Walsingham drew pilgrims for nearly five hundred years, until the suppression of the monasteries by Henry VIII. Ironically, the king had been devoted to the shrine earlier in his reign. He made his first pilgrimage there as king on January 19, 1511, and afterward donated a ruby-encrusted collar and money to glaze the windows of the shrine chapel. In the royal accounts are entries up to the year 1538 recording the annual donation to the shrine of the "King's Candle" and the services of a priest to sing before the statue of Our Lady. In 1536 a visit from royal commissioners, intent on reporting on Walsingham's affairs and preparing the way for its dissolution, fired the first warning shots. During their investigations the men reported that they had found "a secret privy place" in which were strange instruments and pots and potions with which to "divide gold and silver"—implying a secret mint or an alchemist's laboratory. In fact it was almost certainly just a workshop for casting pilgrims' medals and souvenirs.

The end finally came on August 4, 1538, when the shrine was formally surrendered to the Crown. The entry from the king's accounts for September 29 of the same year sums up Walsingham's sudden change of status: "For the King's Candle before Our Lady of Walsingham, and to the Prior there for his salary—Nil." The statue of Our Lady was burned. The priory was sold to a private family, and its church, stripped of lead and pillaged for stone, soon collapsed. As the

Elizabethan ballad expressed it, "Bitter, bitter oh to behold the grass to grow / Where the walls of Walsingham so stately did show."

Now the cycle of history has turned again and the Walsingham Way, the main pilgrimage trail, resounds once more with the tread of pilgrims' feet as Catholics, Anglicans, Orthodox, and other faithful process to the shrines. For Catholics the focus of pilgrimage remains the Slipper Chapel, while for Anglicans the climax of their pilgrimage is the modern shrine church, just north of the old priory wall. Henry VIII and the reformers could destroy the structure, but not the memory of the shrine's devotions; and the memory has been restored to the extent that even Erasmus, the gentle mocker of some aspects of pilgrimage, would surely approve of it.

AFTERWORD

"Every day is a journey, and the journey itself home."

Matsuo Basho

At the end of this book's journey, from ancient shrines of the Old World to sanctuaries in the Americas, we may consider some of the thematic threads and speculate on what direction pilgrimage may take in the future.

At any given period in history, pilgrimage has been subject to the forces of society, for example the prevailing religious beliefs and social mores. Today, pilgrimage in the Western world is experiencing a revival, perhaps partly boosted by secular activities such as sightseeing and hiking.

Sacred journeys to Santiago de Compostela and Taizé (in France) are good examples. Even though the pilgrimage to Santiago de Compostela declined in the early modern world, it was revived in the late twentieth century. Along the Camino, hostels, hotels, shops, and restaurants sprang up or gained a new lease on life. Whole villages were revived. The numbers of pilgrims—which can be estimated by the number of "pilgrims' passports" issued at official pilgrim offices along the route—have increased steadily. In 1985 several hundred pilgrims arrived in Santiago. Subsequent years saw more pilgrims on the Camino; 1993, a Holy Year (and helped by an advertising campaign), drew almost a hundred thousand people. From then on pilgrim numbers have consistently reached five or six figures. In the Holy Year of 2010 more than 270,000 pilgrims made the journey.

Two signs of the renewed popularity of the pilgrimage to Santiago have been the publication of many books about the Camino and the redevelopment of various European walking routes that once brought medieval pilgrims to northwest Spain.

While the journey to Santiago is the tale of a remarkable renewal, the village of Taizé, in Burgundy, represents the successful establishment of a modern pilgrimage. There, in 1940, the Swiss-born Brother Roger Schutz founded an ecumenical community of monks that has evolved into one of the most thriving movements in Western Christendom. Taizé is as much a way of life as it is a pilgrimage destination. During their stay, visitors are encouraged to absorb its values—especially joy, simplicity, and compassion—and its emphasis on quiet reflection, and then return home to put it all into action. Taizé practices what it preaches: a number of its hundred or so brothers, who come from about thirty different countries and from various Christian denominations, live in parts of Africa, Asia, and Latin America, attempting to relate their vision of Christianity to the people around them.

Brother Roger himself was tragically killed in August 2005 at the age of ninety, stabbed by a mentally ill woman in front of some 2,500 people during a Taizé prayer service. People around the world reacted with shock and dismay at the news. But Brother Roger's creation, the community of Taizé, continued with his chosen successor, the German-born Brother Alois, at the helm, celebrating a vision of Christian unity and reaching out, in particular to young people.

Taizé's nonauthoritarian approach to religion, its simple prayers, melodic and repetitive chants, and emphasis that there is more that unites different Christian churches than separates them have added a new dimension to the faith. Thousands of pilgrims, most of them under age thirty, share the Taizé experience each year—sleeping in dormitories or in tents pitched in fields around the village and helping with daily practicalities such as cleaning or preparing food. They attend the daily prayer meetings, participate in discussion groups, meditate in silence, sing together in the candlelit interior of the vast modern Church of Reconciliation, and listen to talks on the Bible given by the brothers. That is Brother Roger's true memorial.

Taizé and Santiago de Compostela are, in their different ways, model contemporary pilgrimage destinations. Yet the phenomenon of pilgrimage, as we have seen, is ancient and draws on innate human spiritual and emotional needs and the hope they will be met by a journey probably involving faith, time for reflection, and hardship. Pilgrimage, in other words, relates directly to the human condition, the "Vale of Soul-Making" as John Keats called it, and as such will likely never go out of fashion.

As pilgrimage in the West has developed in modern times, it has broadened its appeal to those who would not count themselves as spiritual seekers. It has been estimated that a number of the "pilgrims" trekking to Santiago are doing it mainly for the exhilaration of walking and meeting fellow hikers. This in turn raises the question of secular pilgrimage: are nonbelieving participants on a religious pilgrimage such as the Camino or Croagh Patrick true pilgrims? And are those who make a solemn journey to a secular monument, such as a World War cemetery, pilgrims?

In other words, if not defined in strictly religious terms, being a "secular pilgrim" (or spiritual traveler) is a viable concept—taking into account the two elements crucial to pilgrimage: journey and profound transformation. And of course the boundary between the sacred and secular can shift within an individual: a person's feelings of spirituality (or of agnosticism or atheism) can alter during a pilgrimage journey. In the end, only each individual knows if they are spiritual travelers or not, whether they want to be a pilgrim as opposed to a hiker or tourist. And it is important to stress that a person can combine the roles of pilgrim, hiker, and tourist at the same time. We should not deny the nonbeliever moments of "spiritual" wonder on, for example, the slopes of Croagh Patrick, or the committed Christian a moment of agnostic questioning at, say, Fátima or Lourdes.

Another key aspect of modern pilgrimage is the wide choice of destinations: all over the world there are secular historic buildings and sites that can, in the eyes of any thoughtful visitor, become "sacred" destinations and have a similar potency as the shrines and relics of the Middle Ages.

In addition, certain national parks, landscapes, and gardens can have a crowd-drawing magnetism similar to traditional pilgrimage destinations, perhaps offering visitors a sense of nature and freedom and beauty seldom experienced in their everyday lives.

Museums, too, can attract spiritual travelers. The scholars Simon Coleman and John Elsner have noted some of the ways in which they might resemble pilgrimage shrines: for example, museum exhibits are given their own special space, like medieval cathedral relics, and the cases that contain artifacts are equivalent to reliquaries; the various specialist museum rooms are like private chapels; and the architecture of the museum building itself (often in the form of a classical temple) announces that it is a "church of culture."

Perhaps the most radical issue concerning pilgrimage in the twenty-first century is the possibility that, like shopping, you can do it from your armchair. "Virtual pilgrimage" has been made possible by websites and online maps. Via the latter it is now possible to "drive" from, say, Lisbon airport to the shrine of Fátima. On "arrival" at Fátima you can tune in to a webcam positioned in the Chapel of the Apparitions and gaze at the statue of Our Lady of Fátima in real time. A number of pilgrimage shrines now have their own websites offering virtual tours, sometimes accompanied by music, prayers, sacred texts, and the opportunity to buy souvenirs online.

It has been argued that through virtual pilgrimage it is possible to enter the transitional state that is characteristic of physical pilgrimage—that Internet visitors to sacred destinations can be dislocated from their real environment and taken to a sacred realm, accompanied by other "web pilgrims" with whom they can share their experiences through guestbooks.

But although virtual pilgrimage may work as a meditational aid to inner pilgrimage, one commonsense objection to it—apart from the benefits of actual physical exercise and overcoming hardships—is that it is essentially *mediated* pilgrimage. That is to say, a virtual pilgrim participates through images and material of someone else's making.

They are not experiencing the unique sights and sounds and encounters that come with an actual journey to a pilgrim destination. Furthermore, unlike an actual, physical pilgrimage, which involves time in which to reflect and digest, virtual pilgrimage can only attempt to induce states of inner transformation through the instantaneity of mouse clicks or taps. Back in the twelfth century, Pope Alexander III referred to pilgrims journeying so that "in the sweat of their brow and labour of the road, they may avoid the wrath of the heavenly Judge and earn his mercy." Although pilgrimage now seldom reflects the full penitential import of the pope's words, it is difficult to disconnect it entirely from physical effort and the time involved in achieving it.

Despite fluctuations in its popularity, pilgrimage in the Western world has survived some two thousand years, and the indications are that it will continue to thrive in the future—if only because the symbolism of pilgrimage is rooted in the journey of life itself. In short, inasmuch as pilgrimage, with its physical effort and opportunity for spiritual reflection, mirrors the condition of humanity, it is difficult to imagine a future when people will not be setting off on journeys around the world in their search, conscious or unconscious, for help or meaning or peace or "the divine."

NOTES

INTRODUCTION
Epigraph: From Laozi, *Dao De Jing*.

1. WHAT IS PILGRIMAGE?
Epigraph: From Hesse, *Siddhartha*.
10 "and experiencing *communitas*" This is suggested by Turner and Turner in *Image and Pilgrimage in Christian Culture*.

2. SACRED JOURNEYS IN ANCIENT TIMES
Epigraph: In Edelstein and Edelstein, *Asclepius*.
15 "The Greek historian Herodotus" Herodotus's account is in Book II of his *Histories*.
16 "The second-century CE writer Lucian of Samosata" Lucian's account is in *The Syrian Goddess*.
18 "Many of these tablets have survived" The Epidaurus tablet descriptions are in Edelstein and Edelstein, *Asclepius*. I have made a slight alteration to the wording of the translation.
18 "If, as Matthew Dillon has written" In Dillon, *Pilgrims and Pilgrimage in Ancient Greece*.
19 "But as Scott Scullion has pointed out" Scullion's essay is in Elsner and Rutherford (eds.), *Pilgrimage in Graeco-Roman and Early Christian Antiquity*.

3. EARLY PATHS
Epigraph: In Lightfoot, *The Apostolic Fathers*.
23 "the case of the second-century bishop St. Polycarp" In Lightfoot, *The Apostolic Fathers*.
24 "suggested by the fourth-century saint Gregory of Nyssa" Gregory's praise of St. Theodore is in Leemans, Mayer, Allen, and Dehandschutter, *Let Us Die That We May Live*.
25 "a description given by St. Jerome" St. Jerome's experience of the catacombs is told in his *Commentary on Ezekiel*; it is cited by Jonathan Sumption in *Pilgrimage*, a detailed and fascinating account of the pilgrimage experience in the Middle Ages.
26 "'remember your dear Agape'" The Latin inscription, which I have translated, can be found at http://www.newadvent.org/cathen/03417b.htm.

4. THE AGE OF CONSTANTINE
Epigraph: In *The Pilgrimage of the Holy Paula by St. Jerome*.
31 "the anonymous Bordeaux Pilgrim" See Lee, *Pagans and Christians in Late Antiquity*.
31 "the account of a pilgrim named Egeria" See McClure and Feltoe (eds. and trans.), *The Pilgrimage of Etheria*.
33 "Jerome's attitude to the cult of the martyrs" Jerome's letter attacking Vigilantius can be found at http://www.newadvent.org/fathers/3010.htm.

5. CELTS AND ANGLO-SAXONS
Epigraph: From Jonas, *Life of St. Columban*.
37 "'My voice sticks in my throat'" In Jerome's *Letter 127: To Principia*, translated by W. H. Fremantle, G. Lewis, and W. G. Martley. From *Nicene and Post-Nicene Fathers, Second Series*, Vol. 6., edited by Philip Schaff and Henry Wace (Buffalo, 1893). It can be found online at http://www.newadvent.org/fathers/3001127.htm.
41 "Brendan's legendary voyage to the west" See J. F. Webb, *Lives of the Saints*.
46 "English monk and historian Bede" See Bede, *A History of the English Church and People*.
49 "As Kathleen Hughes has noted" Hughes, *The Church in Early Irish Society*.
49 "'There is a heavy toll'" This Old Irish poem was written in the ninth century, apparently by a disappointed pilgrim. My version of the poem, first published in *Oracle Bones*, is from a translation by Whitley Stokes and John Strachan in *Thesaurus Palaeohibernicus*, Vol. 2 (Cambridge, 1903).

6. DECLINE AND REVIVAL
Epigraph: From *The Hodoeporicon of Saint Willibald*.
52 "Arculf traveled to Jerusalem" See Adamnan, *The Pilgrimage of Arculfus in the Holy Land*.

54 "When Bernard the Monk visited the city" In Whalen, *Pilgrimage in the Middle Ages*.

7. THE NEW MILLENNIUM
Epigraph: Glaber's words, here and below, are from Coulton, *Life in the Middle Ages*; I have modernized them slightly.
60 "the *Annals of Nieder-Altaich*" In Whalen, *Pilgrimage in the Middle Ages*.

8. PILGRIMAGE, RELICS, AND THE AFTERLIFE
Epigraph: From Victricius's sermon *De laude sanctorum*; see Victricius of Rouen, "Praising the Saints."
66 "Bede tells the story of a Northumbrian man named Drycthelm" In Book 5 of Bede, *A History of the English Church and People*.
70 "while visiting the monastery of Fécamp in Normandy" In *Magna Vita Sancti Hugonis*.
72 "St. Thomas Aquinas" See *Summa Theologica*, Third Part, Question 25, http://www.newadvent.org/summa/4025.htm.
73 "As Erasmus wrote" See Erasmus, *The Handbook of the Christian Soldier*.

9. ON THE ROAD
Epigraph: From the Nevill Coghill translation.
76 "He anointed the staff and handed it over with the words" See *The Sarum Missal in English*.
77 "When Felix Fabri, during a sermon" Fabri, *The Wanderings of Felix Fabri*.
80 "The twelfth-century *Pilgrim's Guide*" This *Pilgrim's Guide* has been translated into modern English by both James Hogarth and William Melczer.
84 "A time-honored alternative to speech" See Norbert Ohler, *The Medieval Traveller*, which is excellent on the difficulties of communication.

10. ROME
Epigraph: From Gregorius, *The Marvels of Rome*.
89 "Hildebert of Lavardin wrote in a poem" In Parks, *The English Traveller to Italy Vol. 1*.
90 "Alcuin of York said" In Parks, *The English Traveller to Italy Vol. 1*.
95 "according to Peter Partner" Partner, *Renaissance Rome, 1500–1559*.

11. SANTIAGO DE COMPOSTELA
Epigraph: The words from *The Pilgrim's Guide* here and below are from the James Hogarth translation.

12. CANTERBURY
Epigraph: From Erasmus, *The Colloquies, Vol. II*.
108 "they should not make 'a fortress'" See Ward, *The Canterbury Pilgrimages*.

13. JERUSALEM AND THE HOLY LAND
113 "'I cared never for eating, drinking, nor sleeping'" Fabri's words here and below are from Fabri, *The Wanderings of Felix Fabri*. Prescott's extremely readable *Jerusalem Journey* is based on the account of Fabri.

14. CHANGING ATTITUDES
Epigraph: Margery Kempe refers to herself as "she" in her *Book of Margery Kempe*.
121 "a man named William Thorpe" See Jusserand, *English Wayfaring Life in the Middle Ages*; and N. H. Keeble, "Constructing the Protestant Life in Early Modern England," in Morris and Roberts (eds.), *Pilgrimage*.
123 "the *Travels of Sir John Mandeville*" See Pollard (ed.), *The Travels of Sir John Mandeville*.

15. FROM REFORMATION TO ROMANTICISM
Epigraph: In Luther's *To the Christian Nobility*.
126 "Francisco Molina complained" In Hartley, *The Story of Santiago de Compostela*.
126 "Erasmus's 'The Religious Pilgrimage'" In Erasmus, *The Colloquies, Vol. II*.
129 "A contemporary chronicler remarked" Charles Wriothesley, in *A Chronicle of England during the Reigns of the Tudors, from A.D. 1485 to 1559, Vol. 1* (ed. William Douglas Hamilton) (London, 1875).

129 "the Royal Injunctions of 1559" See Frere and Kennedy (eds.), *Visitation Articles and Injunctions of the Period of the Reformation, Vol. III.*

133 "As F. Thomas Noonan has noted" In *The Road to Jerusalem.*

133 "The historian Edward Gibbon" See Volume IV, Chapter 23, of *The History of the Decline and Fall of the Roman Empire.*

136 "Revd. William Gilpin" See *Observations on the River Wye and Several Parts of South Wales.*

16. ORTHODOX PILGRIMAGE
Epigraph: *The Pilgrimage of Joannes Phocas in the Holy Land.*

139 "Daniel of Kiev" See Daniel the Pilgrim, *The Pilgrimage of the Russian Abbot Daniel in the Holy Land.*

141 "Stephen of Novgorod" See Coleman and Elsner, *Pilgrimage*; and Majeska, *Russian Travelers to Constantinople in the Fourteenth and Fifteenth Centuries.*

17. MODERN SHRINES
Epigraph: In Newman, *Parochial and Plain Sermons.*

147 "reputed miraculous apparitions, especially of the Virgin Mary" See Marina Warner, *Alone of All Her Sex.*

149 "in a grotto near her hometown of Lourdes" Ruth Harris, *Lourdes*, is indispensable for the background to Lourdes. See also Houseley and Latham, *A Pilgrim's Guide to Lourdes and the Surrounding Area*; and Kaufman, *Consuming Visions.*

153 "the village of Knock" See Kilcoyne, *Knock . . . and still they come*; and Neary, *I Saw Our Lady.*

157 "the genesis of the village of Fátima" See Haffert, *Meet the Witnesses*; and Madigan, *What Happened at Fatima.*

160 "Scottish folklorist named Alexander Carmichael" See Carmichael, *Carmina Gadelica.*

18. SANCTUARIES IN THE AMERICAS
Epigraph: In Roberts, Donaldson, and Coxe (eds.), *The Ante-Nicene Fathers, Vol. 8.*

161 "Our Lady of Guadalupe in Mexico City" See Anderson and Chávez, *Our Lady of Guadalupe*; and Poole, *Our Lady of Guadalupe.*

163 "the shrine of Sainte-Anne-de-Beaupré" For a good summary of the basilica and its background see Mark Cardwell, *Montreal Gazette*, March 21, 2008.

165 "The town of Chimayo" See Howarth and Lamadrid, *Pilgrimage to Chimayó*; Treib, *Sanctuaries of Spanish New Mexico.*

167 "the Basilica of Our Lady of Aparecida" For a general background, see Fausto, *A Concise History of Brazil*; and Smith, *A History of Brazil.* Bob Walker has given an account of his journey along the Caminho da Fé at http://www.bbc.com/news/magazine-33550932.

19. REVIVING THE PAST
Epigraph: Adomnan (Adamnan) is the principal source for the life of St. Columba.

170 "Ireland's holiest mountain" See Thackeray, *Irish Sketch Book of 1842*; Harry Hughes, *Croagh Patrick.*

171 "In the 1790s a Frenchman" See De Latocnaye, *A Frenchman's Walk through Ireland.*

173 "The tiny island of Iona" See McNeill, *An Iona Anthology* and *Iona*; MacArthur, *Columba's Island*; Marshall, *Iona*; and Millar, *Iona.*

175 "committed to a rule that involves" See Iona Community website, http://iona.org.uk.

177 "In the Middle Ages, Walsingham" See Dickinson, *The Shrine of Our Lady of Walsingham*; Gillett, *Walsingham*; and Martin Warner, *Walsingham.*

177 "Owls do scrike" The ballad is given in full, with modernized spelling, in Bridgett, *Our Lady's Dowry.*

181 "Elizabethan ballad" See Bridgett, *Our Lady's Dowry.*

AFTERWORD
Epigraph: In Basho, *The Narrow Road to the Deep North and Other Travel Sketches.*

184 "the village of Taizé" See Gonzalez Balado, *The Story of Taizé*; Santos, *A Community Called Taizé*; and Spink, *A Universal Heart.*

186 "'Virtual pilgrimage'" Hill-Smith has written on the topic in "Cyberpilgrimage."

BIBLIOGRAPHY

Adair, John, *The Pilgrim's Way: Shrines and Saints in Britain and Ireland* (London, 1978)

Adamnan, *Life of St. Columba* (ed. W. Reeves) (Edinburgh, 1874)

The Pilgrimage of Arculfus in the Holy Land (trans. J. R. Macpherson) (London, 1895)

Alexander, H. G., *Religion in England 1558–1662* (London, 1968)

Anderson, Carl A., and Eduardo Chávez, *Our Lady of Guadalupe: Mother of the Civilization of Love* (New York, 2009)

The Anglo-Saxon Chronicle (London, 1912)

Augustine of Hippo, *The Confessions* (trans. R. S. Pine-Coffin) (New York, 1961)

Bagnoli, Martina, Holger A. Klein, C. Griffith Mann, and James Robinson (eds.), *Treasures of Heaven: Saints, Relics, and Devotion in Medieval Europe* (London, 2011)

Basho, Matsuo, *The Narrow Road to the Deep North and Other Travel Sketches* (trans. Nobuyuki Yuasa) (London, 2005)

Bede, *A History of the English Church and People* (Harmondsworth, 1955)

Benjamin of Tudela, *The Itinerary of Benjamin Tudela* (trans. Marcus Nathan Adler) (London, 1907)

Benson, Robert Hugh, *Lourdes* (London, 1914)

Bhardwaj, Surinder M., *Hindu Places of Pilgrimage in India: A Study in Cultural Geography* (Berkeley, 1973)

Bieler, Ludwig (ed. and trans.), *The Patrician Texts in the Book of Armagh* (Dublin, 1979)

Birch, Debra J., *Pilgrimage to Rome in the Middle Ages: Continuity and Change* (Woodbridge, 1998)

Bridgett, T. E., *Our Lady's Dowry* (New York and London, 1875)

Brown, Peter, *The Cult of the Saints: Its Rise and Function in Latin Christianity* (London, 1981)

Bunyan, John, *The Pilgrim's Progress* (Harmondsworth, 1965)

Butcher, Kevin, *Roman Syria and the Near East* (London, 2003)

Carmichael, Alexander, *Carmina Gadelica: Hymns and Incantations from the Gaelic* (New York, 1992)

Catholic Encyclopedia (New York, 1907–14)

Chadwick, Henry, *The Early Church* (rev. ed.) (London, 1993)

Chateaubriand, François-René de, *Travels to Jerusalem and the Holy Land, through Egypt* (London, 1835)

Chaucer, Geoffrey, *The Canterbury Tales* (trans. Nevill Coghill) (Harmondsworth, 1951)

Coleman, Simon, and John Elsner, *Pilgrimage: Past and Present in the World Religions* (London, 1995)

Cook's Tourists' Handbook for Palestine and Syria (London, 1876)

Coulton, C. G., *Life in the Middle Ages* (Cambridge, 1910)

Cragg, G. R., *The Church and the Age of Reason, 1648–1789* (Harmondsworth, 1960)

Daniel the Pilgrim, *The Pilgrimage of the Russian Abbot Daniel in the Holy Land: 1106–1107* (ed. C. W. Wilson) (London, 1895)

Davidson, Linda Kay, and David M. Gitlitz, *Pilgrimage: From the Ganges to Graceland: An Encyclopedia* (Santa Barbara, 2002)

Davies, Horton, and Marie-Hélène Davies, *Holy Days and Holidays: The Medieval Pilgrimage to Compostela* (London and Toronto, 1982)

Dawe, Donald, "The Blessed Virgin in Depth Psychology: A Theological Appraisal," in McLoughlin, William, and Jill Pinnock (eds.), *Mary is for Everyone: Essays on Mary and Ecumenism* (Leominster, 1997)

De Latocnaye, Chevalier, *A Frenchman's Walk through Ireland, 1796–7* (trans. John Stevenson) (Belfast, 1917)

Dickinson, J. C., *The Shrine of Our Lady of Walsingham* (Cambridge, 1956)

Dillon, Matthew, *Pilgrims and Pilgrimage in Ancient Greece* (reprint edition) (London, 2012)

Duffy, Eamon, *The Stripping of the Altars: Traditional Religion in England c. 1400–c. 1580* (New Haven and London, 1992)

Eck, Diana L., *Banaras: City of Light* (2nd ed.) (New York, 1999)

Edelstein, E. J., and L. Edelstein, *Asclepius: Collection and Interpretation of the Testimonies* (Baltimore and London, 1998)

Elsner, Jas, and Ian Rutherford (eds.), *Pilgrimage in Graeco-Roman and Early Christian Antiquity: Seeing the Gods* (Oxford, 2005)

Erasmus, Desiderius, *The Colloquies, Vol. II* (trans. N. Bailey) (London, 1900)
The Handbook of the Christian Soldier, in *The Erasmus Reader* (ed. Erika Rummel) (Toronto, 1990)

Fabri, Felix, *The Wanderings of Felix Fabri* (trans. Aubrey Stewart) (London, 1892–97)

Fausto, Boris, *A Concise History of Brazil* (Cambridge, 1999)

Fedden, Robert, *Syria: An Historical Appreciation* (London, 1955)

Field, Victoria, *Baggage: A Book of Leavings* (London, 2016)

Finlay, Ian, *Columba* (Glasgow, 1990)

Finucane, R. C., *Miracles and Pilgrims: Popular Beliefs in Medieval England* (London, 1977)

Fletcher, Richard, *The Conversion of Europe: From Paganism to Christianity, 371–1386 AD* (London, 1998)

Freeman, Charles, *Holy Bones, Holy Dust: How Relics Shaped the History of Medieval Europe* (New Haven and London, 2012)

Frere, W. H., and W. M. Kennedy (eds.), *Visitation Articles and Injunctions of the Period of the Reformation, Vol. III, 1559–1575* (London, 1910)

Geary, Patrick J., *Furta Sacra: Thefts of Relics in the Central Middle Ages* (rev. ed.) (Princeton, 1991)

Gibbon, Edward, *The History of the Decline and Fall of the Roman Empire* (reprint) (Ware, 1998)

Gillett, H. M., *Walsingham: The History of a Famous Shrine* (London, 1950)

Gilpin, William, *Observations on the River Wye and Several Parts of South Wales* (London, 1782)

Gonzalez Balado, J. L., *The Story of Taizé* (London, 1980)

Graham, Stephen, *With the Russian Pilgrims to Jerusalem* (London, 1913)

Gregorius, Master, *The Marvels of Rome* (trans. John Osborne) (Toronto, 1987)

Green, V. H. H., *Luther and the Reformation* (London, 1964)

Haffert, John M., *Meet the Witnesses* (Fatima, 1961)

Håland, Evy Johanne, "The Dormition of the Virgin Mary on the Island of Tinos: A Performance of Gendered Values in Greece," in *Journal of Religious History*, Vol. 36, no. 1, March 2012

Hanbury-Tenison, Robin, *Spanish Pilgrimage: A Canter to St James* (London, 1990)

Harbison, Peter, *Pilgrimage in Ireland: The Monuments and the People* (London, 1991)

Hardy, Philip Dixon, *Holy Wells of Ireland* (London, 1840)

Harpur, James, *Love Burning in the Soul: The Story of the Christian Mystics, from Saint Paul to Thomas Merton* (Boston, 2005)
Oracle Bones (London, 2001)

Harratt, George, *Scattery Island: A Guide to its History and Buildings* (Kilrush, 1995)

Harris, Ruth, *Lourdes: Body and Spirit in the Secular Age* (London, 1999)

Harris, Walter, *The Ancient and Present State of the County of Down* (Dublin, 1744)

Hartley, C. G., *The Story of Santiago de Compostela* (London, 1912)

Heath, Sidney, *In the Steps of the Pilgrims* (London, 1950)

Henson, Robert Hugh, *Lourdes* (London, 1914)

Herodotus, *The Histories* (trans. Aubrey de Selincourt) (London and New York, 1996)

Hesse, Hermann, *Siddhartha* (London, 2008)

Hetherington, Paul, *Medieval Rome: A Portrait of the City and Its Life* (London, 1994)

Hibbert, Christopher, *The Grand Tour* (London, 1987)

Hill-Smith, Connie, "Cyberpilgrimage: A Study of Authenticity, Presence and Meaning in Online Pilgrimage Experiences," in *Journal of Religion and Popular Culture*, Vol. 21, no. 2, Summer 2009

The Hodoeporicon of Saint Willibald (trans. W. R. Brownlow) (London, 1895)

Hopkins, Keith, *A World Full of Gods: Pagans, Jews and Christians in the Roman Empire* (London, 2000)

Houseley, David, and Peter Latham, *A Pilgrim's Guide to Lourdes and the Surrounding Area* (2nd. ed.) (Woodbridge, 2011)

Howarth, Sam, and Enrique R. Lamadrid, *Pilgrimage to Chimayó: Contemporary Portrait of a Living Tradition* (Santa Fe, 1999)

Hoyle, Peter, *Delphi* (London, 1967)

Hughes, Harry, *Croagh Patrick: A Place of Pilgrimage, A Place of Beauty* (Dublin, 2010)

Croagh Patrick: A Place of Ancient Pilgrimage (Westport, 1991)

Hughes, Kathleen, *The Church in Early Irish Society* (London, 1966)

"The Changing Theory and Practice of Irish Pilgrimage," in *The Journal of Ecclesiastical History*, Vol. 11, no. 2, 1960

Hunt, E. D., *Holy Land Pilgrimage in the Later Roman Empire, AD 312–460* (Oxford, 1982)

Ibn Battuta, *Travels in Asia and Africa 1325–1354* (trans. and ed. H. A. R. Gibb) (London, 1929)

Jackson, Bernard, *Places of Pilgrimage* (London, 1989)

Jonas, *Life of St. Columban* (ed. Dana Carleton Munro) (Philadelphia, 1895)

Jung, Carl G., *Answer to Job* (2nd. ed.) (Princeton, 1969)

Jusserand, J., *English Wayfaring Life in the Middle Ages* (London, 1889)

Kaufman, Suzanne K., *Consuming Visions: Mass Culture and the Lourdes Shrine* (New York, 2005)

Kempe, Margery, *The Book of Margery Kempe* (ed. W. Butler-Bowdon) (London, 1936)

Kempis, Thomas à, *The Imitation of Christ* (trans. Leo Sherley-Price) (Harmondsworth, 1952)

Kendall, Alan, *Medieval Pilgrims* (London, 1970)

Kilcoyne, Colm, *Knock . . . and still they come* (Dublin, 2012)

Knight, Cher Krause, "Mickey, Minnie, and Mecca: Destination Disney World, Pilgrimage in the Twentieth Century," in *Reclaiming the Spiritual in Art* (eds. Dawn Perlmutter and Debra Koppman) (New York, 1999)

Knox, E. A., *John Bunyan* (London, 1928)

Langland, William, *Piers Plowman* (trans. A. V. C. Schmidt) (Oxford, 1992)

Lee, A. D., *Pagans and Christians in Late Antiquity: A Sourcebook* (London, 2000)

Leemans, Johan, Wendy Mayer, Pauline Allen, and Boudewijn Dehandschutter, *Let Us Die That We May Live: Greek Homilies on Christian Martyrs from Asia Minor, Palestine and Syria (c. AD 350–AD 450)* (London and New York, 2003)

Lehane, Brendan, *Early Celtic Christianity* (London, 1968)

Lightfoot, J. B., *The Apostolic Fathers, Part II*, "S. Ignatius, S. Polycarp" (3 vols., 2nd ed.) (London, 1889)

Lochtefeld, James G., *God's Gateway: Identity and Meaning in a Hindu Pilgrimage Place* (New York and Oxford, 2010)

Louth, Andrew, *Introducing Eastern Orthodox Theology* (London, 2013)

Luard, Nicholas, *The Field of the Star: A Pilgrim's Journey to Santiago de Compostela* (London, 1998)

Lucian of Samosata, *The Syrian Goddess* (trans. Herbert A. Strong and ed. John Garstang) (London, 1913)

Lukatis, Ingrid, "Church Meetings and Pilgrimages in Germany," in *Social Compass*, 36, no. 2 (1989), quoted in Coleman, Simon, and John Elsner, *Pilgrimage: Past and Present in the World Religions* (London, 1995) (p. 128)

Luther, Martin, *To the Christian Nobility*, in *Luther's Works, Vol. 44* (eds. J. J. Pelikan, H. C. Oswald, and H. T. Lehmann) (Philadelphia, 1966)

MacArthur, E. Mairi, *Columba's Island: Iona from Past to Present* (rev. ed.) (Edinburgh, 2007)

Madigan, Leo, *What Happened at Fatima* (London, 2000)

Magna Vita Sancti Hugonis (eds. Decima L. Douie and D. H. Farmer) (Oxford, 1985)

Majeska, George P., *Russian Travelers to Constantinople in the Fourteenth and Fifteenth Centuries* (Washington, D.C., 1984)

Markides, Kyriacos C., *The Mountain of Silence: A Search for Orthodox Spirituality* (New York, 2002)

Marshall, Rosalind K., *Iona: A New History* (Dingwall, 2013)

Martin, Sally, *Every Pilgrim's Guide to Lourdes* (Norwich, 2005)

Masson, Georgina, *The Companion Guide to Rome* (London, 1965)

McClure, M. L., and C. L. Feltoe (eds. and trans.), *The Pilgrimage of Etheria* (London, 1919)

McGuckin, John Anthony, *The Orthodox Church: An Introduction to Its History, Doctrine, and Spiritual Culture* (Oxford, 2011)

McNeill, F. Marian, *An Iona Anthology* (Iona, 1990)
Iona: A History of the Island (London, 1959)

Michell, George, *The Penguin Guide to the Monuments of India, Volume 1: Buddhist, Jain, Hindu* (London, 1989)

Michell, John, *The Traveller's Key to Sacred England* (New York, 1988)

Millar, Peter, *Iona: A Pilgrim's Guide* (Norwich, 2007)

Miller, William, *Mediaeval Rome* (London, 1901)

Mirabilia Urbis Romae (trans. Francis Morgan Nichols) (Rome, 1889)

Mitchell, Nathan, *The Mystery of the Rosary: Marian Devotion and the Reinvention of Catholicism* (New York, 2009)

Montefiore, Simon Sebag, *Jerusalem: The Biography* (London, 2012)

Morris, Colin, and Peter Roberts (eds.), *Pilgrimage: The English Experience from Becket to Bunyan* (Cambridge, 2002)

Morton, W. Scott, *Japan: Its History and Culture* (Newton Abbot, 1975)

Mullins, Edwin, *The Pilgrimage to Santiago* (London, 1974)

Neame, Alan, *The Happening at Lourdes* (London, 1968)

Neary, Tom, *I Saw Our Lady* (Knock, 1995)

Neillands, Rob, *The Road to Compostela* (Ashbourne, 1985)

Newman, John Henry, *Parochial and Plain Sermons* (San Francisco, 1997)

Ní Mheara, Róisín, *In Search of Irish Saints: The Peregrinatio Pro Christo* (Blackrock, 1994)

Noonan, F. Thomas, *The Road to Jerusalem: Pilgrimage and Travel in the Age of Discovery* (Philadelphia, 2007)

Noy, David, "Rabbi Aqiba Comes to Rome: A Jewish Pilgrimage in Reverse?" in Elsner, Jas, and Ian Rutherford (eds.), *Pilgrimage in Graeco-Roman and Early Christian Antiquity: Seeing the Gods* (Oxford, 2005)

Ohler, Norbert, *The Medieval Traveller* (trans. Caroline Hillier) (Woodbridge, 1989)

O'Laverty, James, *An Historical Account of the Diocese of Down and Connor, Ancient and Modern, Vol. 1* (Dublin, 1878)

Parke, H. W., *Greek Oracles* (London, 1967)

Parks, G. B., *The English Traveller to Italy Vol. 1: The Middle Ages* (Rome, 1954)

Partner, Peter, *Renaissance Rome, 1500–1559: A Portrait of a Society* (Berkeley, 1979)

Pausanias, *Guide to Greece: Central Greece* (trans. Peter Levi) (Harmondsworth, 1979)

The Pilgrimage of Joannes Phocas in the Holy Land (trans. Aubrey Stewart) (London, 1896)

The Pilgrimage of the Holy Paula by St. Jerome (trans. Aubrey Stewart) (London, 1887)

The Pilgrim's Guide: A 12th-Century Guide for the Pilgrim to St. James of Compostella (trans. James Hogarth) (London, 1992)

The Pilgrim's Guide to Santiago de Compostela (trans. William Melczer) (New York, 1993)

Pollard, A. W. (ed.), *The Travels of Sir John Mandeville* (New York, 1900)

Poole, Stafford, *Our Lady of Guadalupe: The Origins and Sources of a Mexican National Symbol, 1531–1797* (Tucson, 1996)

Popham, Peter, *Wooden Temples of Japan* (London, 1990)

Prescott, H. F. M., *Jerusalem Journey: Pilgrimage to the Holy Land in the Fifteenth Century* (London, 1954)

Ridgeon, Lloyd (ed.), *Major World Religions: From Their Origins to the Present* (London and New York, 2003)

Robb, Graham, *The Ancient Paths: Discovering the Lost Map of Celtic Europe* (London, 2013)

Roberts, Alexander, James Donaldson, and A. Cleveland Coxe (eds.), *The Ante-Nicene Fathers, Vol. 8* (Buffalo, 1886)

Santos, Jason Brian, *A Community Called Taizé* (Downers Grove, 2008)

The Sarum Missal in English (trans. A. H. Pearson) (London, 1868)

Scullion, Scott, "Pilgrimage and Greek Religion: Sacred and Secular in the Pagan Polis," in Elsner, Jas, and Ian Rutherford (eds.), *Pilgrimage in Graeco-Roman and Early Christian Antiquity: Seeing the Gods* (Oxford, 2005)

Severin, Tim, *The Brendan Voyage: Across the Atlantic in a Leather Boat* (Dublin, 2005)

Seward, Desmond, *The Dancing Sun: Journeys to the Miracle Shrines* (London, 1993)

Shearer, Alistair, *The Traveller's Key to Northern India* (London, 1987)

Smith, Jeffrey Chipps, *Sensuous Worship: Jesuits and the Art of the Early Catholic Reformation in Germany* (Princeton, 2002)

Smith, Joseph, *A History of Brazil* (London, 2002)

Snowden Ward, H., *The Canterbury Pilgrimages* (London, 1927)

Speake, Graham, *Mount Athos: Renewal in Paradise* (New Haven and London, 2004)

Spink, Kathryn, *A Universal Heart: The Life and Vision of Brother Roger of Taizé* (rev. ed.) (London, 2005)

Stephens, John Lloyd, *Incidents of Travel in Egypt, Arabia Petraea, and the Holy Land* Volume II (New York, 1838)

Stevenson, James, *The Catacombs: Rediscovered Monuments of Early Christianity* (London, 1978)

Stokes, Whitley (ed. and trans.), *The Tripartite Life of Patrick* (London, 1887)

Sumption, Jonathan, *Pilgrimage: An Image of Mediaeval Religion* (London, 1975)

The Syrian Goddess (trans. Herbert A. Strong) (London, 1913)

Taylor, J. E., *Christians and the Holy Places: The Myth of Jewish-Christian Origins* (Oxford, 1993)

Thackeray, William Makepeace, *Irish Sketch Book of 1842* (New York, 1911)

Thomas, Keith, *Religion and the Decline of Magic: Studies in Popular Beliefs in Sixteenth- and Seventeenth-Century England* (London, 1991)

Treib, Marc, *Sanctuaries of Spanish New Mexico* (Berkeley, 1993)

Turner, V., and E. Turner, *Image and Pilgrimage in Christian Culture* (New York, 1978)

Twain, Mark, *The Innocents Abroad* (reprint) (Ware, 2010)

Varner, Gary R., *Sacred Wells: A Study in the History, Meaning, and Mythology of Holy Wells and Waters* (New York, 2009)

Victricius of Rouen, "Praising the Saints" (trans. Gillian Clark), in *Journal of Early Christian Studies*, Vol. 7, no. 3, 1999

Walsh, William Thomas, *Our Lady of Fatima* (New York, 1990)

Ward, Henry Snowden, *The Canterbury Pilgrimages* (London, 1904)

Ware, Timothy, *The Orthodox Church* (2nd. ed.) (London, 1993)

Warner, Marina, *Alone of All Her Sex: The Myth and the Cult of the Virgin Mary* (2nd. ed.) (Oxford, 2013)

Warner, Martin, *Walsingham: An Ever-Circling Year* (Oxford, 1996)

The Way of a Pilgrim (trans. R. M. French) (London, 1942)

Webb, Diana, *Pilgrims and Pilgrimage in the Medieval West* (London, 1999)

Webb, J. F., *Lives of the Saints: The Voyage of St Brendan; Bede: Life of Cuthbert; Eddius Stephanus: Life of Wilfrid* (Harmondsworth, 1965)

Westwood, Jennifer, *Sacred Journeys* (London, 1997)

Whalen, Brett Edward, *Pilgrimage in the Middle Ages: A Reader* (Toronto, 2011)

Wilkinson, John, *Jerusalem Pilgrims Before the Crusades* (Warminster, 1972)

Jerusalem Pilgrimage 1099–1185 (London, 1988)

Williams, Wes, *Pilgrimage and Narrative in the French Renaissance* (Oxford, 1998)

Yelton, Michael, *Alfred Hope Patten: The Shrine of Our Lady at Walsingham* (Norwich, 2006)

INDEX

Abeyta, Don Bernardo, 166
Abraham, 9, 44
Acheiropita, 93
Adam of Usk, 90, 91
Address to the Christian Nobility of the German Nation (Luther), 128
Adomnan, 52, 176, 177
Adonis, cult of, 16
Aelfsige, 91
Aeneid (Virgil), 26, 66
Agen (France), 70–71
Agiulf, 93
Aidan, 48
Albert of Mainz, 127
Alcetas of Helieis, 18
Alcuin of York, 54, 90
Aldhelm, 98
Alexander III, 79, 108, 187
Alexander VI, 95
Alfonso II, 98–99
Alfred the Great, 56
al-Hakim, 60
Allucius of Pescia, 80
Alps, 31, 80, 82, 90–91, 134, 136
Altamira (Spain), 12
Ambrosia of Athens, 19
Amiens (France), 87
Anacharsis, 118
Angers (France), 71
Angles, 38, 39, 46
Anglo-Saxon Chronicle, 41, 56
Anglo-Saxons, 46, 47
Annals of Nieder-Altaich, 60–61
Annals of Ulster, 171
Anne (mother of Mary), 163–65
Annegray (France), 44
Antioch, 32, 33, 36
Antony of Egypt, 35–36
Aparecida, 167–68
Aphrodite, 16
Apollo, 14, 17
apparition(s), 8, 92, 147–60, 161–62, 178
Aquinas, Thomas. *See* Thomas Aquinas
Arcadius, 33
Arculf, 52–53
Argyll, eighth duke of, 175, 177
Arian heresy, 30
Arles (France), 100
ar-Rashid, Harun, 54
Arthur, 100
Arundel, Thomas, 121
asceticism, 35–36, 106
Asclepius, 2, 18
Assumptionists, 151
Astarte, 16

Astorga (Spain), 101
Athanasius, 35
Aubert, 55
Augustine of Canterbury, 46–47, 71, 105
Augustine of Hippo, 10, 67, 72, 123–24
Augustulus, Romulus, 38
Avebury, 13–14
Avignon, 90, 120

"Babylonian captivity," 90, 120
Badudegn, 48–49
Bangor (Ireland), 40, 44
Barking (England), 48
Bastet-Artemis, 15
Beauraing (Belgium), 147
Becket, Thomas, 71, 78, 105–11, 134
  assassination of, 105, 108
  cult of, 108, 111
  life of, 106–8
  miracles linked to, 108, 109
  relics of, 109, 110
  shrine of, 71, 78, 109, 111, 134
  tomb of, 108–9
Bede, 46, 47–48, 66, 71, 170–71
bedouins, 60, 79, 115, 117
Benedictine rule, 49, 57, 82
Bernard of Menthon, 91
Bernard the Monk, 52, 54–55
Bethany, 31, 34
Bethlehem, 21, 32, 33, 34, 55, 117, 139
Bible
  English translation of, 121
  mountains in, as sacred places, 15
Black Death, 94, 119–20. *See also* plague
Black Madonna, 146, 167
Bobbio (Italy), 44, 45, 90
Boccacio, 73
Boniface, 47
Boniface VIII, 69, 120
Boniface IX, 69
Book of Armagh, 170
Book of Margery Kempe (Kempe), 122
Bordeaux Pilgrim, 31, 38
Borgia, Rodrigo, 95
Bosio, Antonio, 27
Boswell, James, 135
Boubastis (Egypt), 15–16, 19
Boxley (England), 110
Boyd, Charlotte, 177–78
Brannock, 179

Brendan of Clonfert (the Navigator), 41–44
Brendan Voyage, The (Severin), 42–43
Breuil (France), 45
Breviarius, 35
Bridget of Sweden, 68
Bromholm (England), 63, 70
Bunyan, John, 7, 132–33
burial rituals, 24–25
Butler, Joseph, 133
Byblos, 16, 19
Byrne, Dominick, 157
Byrne, Mary, 154, 156
Byzantine Empire, 51, 114, 138
Byzantium, 30. *See also* Constantinople

Caedwalla, 48, 90
Calvin, John, 128
Camino de Santiago, 100–2, 183–84, 185. *See also* Santiago de Compostela
Camino Francés, 100, 101
  pilgrim routes in France, 100–1
Campbell, Judith, 155
Cana, 34, 139
Canaan, 9
candles, healing and, 86–87
Canterbury, 71, 79, 86, 87, 105–11, 122, 125, 126, 127, 169, 173, 177
  Becket and, 105, 106, 111
  legends associated with, 106
  pilgrimage to, 105–6, 111, 125, 127
  routes to, 110
Canterbury Tales (Chaucer), 63, 73, 83, 109–10, 122
Canterbury water, 87, 106
Capernaum, 30, 34
Carmichael, Alexander, 160
Carnac (France), 12–13, 14
Carolingian Empire, 49
Casimir, John, 146
catacombs, 25–27, 67, 91, 148
cathedrals, sensory experience of, 84–85
Catherine of Alexandria, 139–40
Catherine of Aragon, 128
Cavanagh (archdeacon), 155
cave paintings, 12
Celestine, 40
Celsus, 72
Celts (Celtic), 11, 39, 45, 46, 47, 173
cemeteries, 24–25

corruption of, 95
Great Schism and, 120
moved to Avignon, 90, 120
prestige of, and pilgrimage,
89–90
pardoners, 69, 73
Paris, 45, 46, 56, 62, 79, 85, 100,
134, 147
Sainte-Chapelle, 62
Partner, Peter, 95
Patmos, 139, 140
Patrick, 40
Patten, Alfred Hope, 178
Paul, 9–10, 22, 26–27, 67, 87,
89, 92, 127, 143
Paul (prior), 115, 117
Paul I, 27
Paula, 33–34
Paul the Deacon, 54
Paul the Hermit, 42
Paulinus of Nola, 30
Pavia (Italy), 90, 91
Peace of Augsburg, 128
"Peace of God" movement, 57
Peace of Westphalia, 132
Pecham, 67
Pelerin de Lorete (Richeome), 131
penance, 1, 67–69, 160
Penitential (Egbert), 68
Penitentials, 68
peregrinus (*peregrini*), 6, 130
English, 47–49
Irish, 6, 8, 40–41, 43, 44, 45,
49, 99, 143, 176
Péronne (France), 46
Persia, 51
Peter, 26–27, 55, 87, 89, 90, 93,
116, 126
Peter of Pisa, 54
Peyramale (priest), 149–50
Philip IV, 120
Phocas, John, 138–39
Phoenicia, 15, 16
phrase books, 84
Piacenza (Italy), 90, 91
Picaud, Aimery, 100, 101
Picts, 176
pilgrimage. *See also* pilgrims
as act of imagination, 131
alternative approaches to, 130,
134–36
alternatives to, for penance,
68, 69
badges, 87–88, 94, 97, 102,
111
on behalf of the deceased, 68
Charlemagne improving
conditions for, 54
Crusades linked with, 61–62
decline in, 3, 121, 125–36
Eastern Orthodox tradition
for, 137–43

etymology of, 6
faith and, 5
food during, 76, 77, 81, 84,
101, 114, 118
funding for, 77
guidebooks, 91, 92–93, 122,
130
historical evidence for, 11–12
inner journey of, 7, 131, 139,
142, 186
languages used on, 84
lodging during, 77, 82–84,
110, 116. *See also* hospices;
hostels; inns
opposition to, 121–22,
125–26
out of fashion in post-
Reformation Europe, 133
as penance, 67–68
preparation for, 75–77
reasons and motives for, 1, 7,
8, 9, 10, 65, 90, 124, 141
reformers' damage to, 128–29
revival of, 3–4, 146, 169–81,
183–85
sea voyages, 33, 41–44, 45,
52, 80–81, 114, 115, 118,
176
secular, 4, 130, 185–86
shrine(s). *See* shrine(s)
stages of, 1–2
tokens left at sites. *See*
offering(s)
virtual, 186–87
Pilgrimage of the Life of Man
(Deguileville), 132
pilgrims. *See also* pilgrimage
clothes and accessories for, 1,
76–77, 102
dangers facing, 7, 79–81
emotions of, on arrival,
84–85, 116
food for, 76, 77, 81, 84, 101,
114
hoping for a cure, 1, 8, 23,
44, 48, 85, 86, 130, 142,
151, 153, 156, 164, 165,
166
legal protection for, 76
lodgings for, 57, 77, 82–84,
110, 116. *See also* hospices;
hostels; inns
money for, 77
motives of, 1, 7, 8, 9, 10, 65,
124, 141
offerings of, 2, 21–22, 77,
86–87
package tours for, 114
passports for, 75–76
protection for, 57, 76
provisions for, 52, 81
rivers, as impediments,

79–80
send-offs for, 77–78
transportation for, 78–81,
114, 146
visual reward for, 72
Pilgrim's Guide (12th c.), 80, 82,
85, 100–3
Pilgrim's Progress, The (Bunyan),
7, 132–33
Pilgrim's Way (England), 79
pillar hermits, 36
Pippin II, 47
pirates, 40, 56, 57, 81, 114
Pisa, 56, 90
Pisa (church council), 120
Pius IX, 148
Pius X, 163
Pius XI, 167
plague, 38, 72, 119–20
plenary indulgences. *See*
indulgences
Polycarp of Smyrna, 23–24
Ponferrada (Spain), 102
Pontmain (France), 147
Preseli Hills, 14
Prester John, 123
Proserpine (Persephone), 16
Protestant Reformation. *See*
Reformation
Prudentius, 27
Puente la Reina (Spain), 101
purgatory, 3, 26, 48, 65, 73, 102,
127, 129
biblical justification for, 66–67
time spent in, 68–69
Puritans, 132
Pyrenees, 82, 97, 100, 101, 149
Pythia, 17

Quebec City, 163, 164

Raleigh, Walter, 77
Reformation, 2, 3, 33, 63, 70, 73,
95, 105, 125–30, 145, 148,
175, 177, 180
relics, 3, 8, 22, 23, 32, 35, 46, 48,
52, 61, 69, 85, 86, 87, 88,
97, 101, 109, 126, 127, 128,
132, 135, 136, 137, 140,
141, 142, 147, 169, 186
authenticity of, 72, 126
broken up, after the
Reformation, 129–30
cult of, 3, 22, 65, 169
demand for, 70–72
display of, 73
healings and, 48, 85
importance of, in medieval
life, 70–71
in Jerusalem, 30, 32, 52, 113,
116–17
miracles and, 63

ACKNOWLEDGMENTS

I'd like to thank a number of people who have helped in the making of this book. My publisher Jan-Erik Guerth has been a constant support and enthusiastic fellow pilgrim; Vicky Field was kind enough to lead me to an Orthodox guide, Father Benedict Ramsden; Eveline O'Donovan applied her eagle eyes to the text and gave me encouragement throughout.